Make Your Own Darn Good Cookies

Cookies, Biscotti, Coffee, and Other Comfort Food

by Donald P. Scoby

Text copyright © 2016-2018 by Donald Patrick Scoby
Nature photography copyright © 2016 by Cara Lynnae Hefflinger
Clan MacDonald Cup photo copyright © 2014 Eryn Galloway
Bigfoot and Chupacabra illustrations copyright © 2017 Linda Luhman
How-To photography and other assorted pictures copyright © 2018 by Brian Smith
BagpiperDon photo copyright © 2013 Chris Terrell
Double Chocolate Biscotti photo copyright © 2017 Arne O. Sandness
All other photography copyright © 2014-2018 by Donald Patrick Scoby
All trademarks and copyrighted items mentioned and shown in photos are the property of their respective owners.
All rights reserved. No part of this book may be reproduced or transmitted in whole or in part in any form or by any means, electronic or mechanical, including photocopying, recording, or by any information storage and retrieval system, except for brief quotations embodied in critical articles or reviews, without written permission from the author.

In perpetuity throughout the universe.

ISBN-10: 1727595521
ISBN-13: 978-1727595529
Imprint: Independently published

Make Your Own Darn Good Cookies

Cookies, Biscotti, Coffee, and Other Comfort Food

by Donald P. Scoby
Owner of Whidbey Island Baking Company

~ To Rene with my Gratitude ~

For her Vision that started WIBC,

Encouragement since Day One,

and Inspiration to write my First Book.

TABLE OF CONTENTS

INTRODUCTION I

MEASUREMENT CONVERSIONS & INGREDIENT NAMES IX

COOKIE SQUARES 1

ALMOND CRANBERRY COOKIE SQUARES 5
BRUNETTIE COOKIE SQUARES 7
BUTTERSCOTCH BLONDIE COFFEE COOKIE SQUARES 9
CHOCOLATE PEPPERMINT COOKIE SQUARES 12
CRANBERRY ORANGE COOKIE SQUARES 14
DIRTY BLONDIE COOKIE SQUARES 16
DOUBLE CHOCOLATE COOKIE SQUARES 18
ESPRESSO CHOCOLATE CHIP COOKIE SQUARES 20
LEMON COOKIE SQUARES 22
MINT CHOCOLATE CHIP COOKIE SQUARES 25
STRAWBERRY LEMONADE COOKIE SQUARES 28
COOKIE SQUARES REFERENCE 30
CHOCOLATE CITRUS COOKIE SQUARES 30
CHOCOLATE RASPBERRY COOKIE SQUARES 31
LEMON CITRUS COOKIE SQUARES 31
LEMON LIME COOKIE SQUARES 31
LEMON RASPBERRY COOKIE SQUARES 31
HOW TO SPREAD COOKIE SQUARES 32
HOW TO CUT COOKIE SQUARES 40
HOW TO CUT DIAMOND SHAPED COOKIE SQUARES 58

BISCOTTI 79

ANISE BISCOTTI 83
ANISE-ALMOND BISCOTTI 86
CRANBERRY ORANGE BISCOTTI 89
DOUBLE CHOCOLATE BISCOTTI 92
ESPRESSO BISCOTTI 95
GINGER CITRUS BISCOTTI 98
LEMON CAKE BISCOTTI 101

PEANUT BUTTER BISCOTTI 105
PUMPKIN PIE BISCOTTI 108
TOASTED ALMOND BISCOTTI 112
BISCOTTI REFERENCE 115
CHOCOLATE CITRUS BISCOTTI 117
CHOCOLATE PEPPERMINT BISCOTTI 118
CHOCOLATE RASPBERRY BISCOTTI 118
LEMON CITRUS BISCOTTI 118
LEMON LIME BISCOTTI 118
ALMOND CHOCOLATE MARBLE BISCOTTI 121
MOCHA MARBLE BISCOTTI 121
TIGER EYE BISCOTTI 121
HOW TO ROLL BISCOTTI 122
HOW TO ROLL BISCOTTI IN NUTS 140
HOW TO CUT BISCOTTI 158

MORE COOKIES 171

THE ORIGINAL BIGFOOT MONSTER COOKIE 175
THE ORIGINAL CHUPACABRA MONSTER COOKIE 178
COWBOY COOKIES 181
SCOTTISH SHORTBREAD 183
WRINKLES 187
MORE COOKIES REFERENCE 189

COFFEE, COFFEE CAKE, AND APPLESAUCE 191

HOW TO MAKE GREAT COFFEE USING A FRENCH PRESS 197
FLAVOURED COFFEE 202
SIMPLE PUMPKIN SPICE LATTE 204
RUSSIAN TEA 205
FRIENDSHIP TEA 206
BLUEBERRY BUCKLE 207
EASY SLOW COOKER APPLESAUCE 210

MAIN COURSES 213

CHRIS & ARNE'S FABULOUS CHEESEBURGER SOUP 217

CHRIS & ARNE'S FABULOUS CHICKEN-BACON BURGER SOUP 220
INCREDIBLE BAKED ZITI 223
SIMPLE SLOW COOKER PULLED PORK........................225
SLOW COOKER TACO SOUP 227

HIGHLAND BAGPIPE SHEET MUSIC............................231

BEAG AIR BHEAG (LITTLE BY LITTLE) 234
LULLABY FOR ZOË 236
BROTHER EMMETT'S WALTZ 238

ABOUT THE AUTHOR 241

OTHER WORKS AND FUTURE WORK..........................242

INTRODUCTION

Thank You for picking up a copy of my debut Whidbey Island Baking Company recipe book!

Whidbey Island Baking Company officially launched as a commercial bakery on a snowy morning December 1, 2014, in Clinton, Washington. I immediately began supplying my unique biscotti and signature cookies to select island grocery stores and restaurants; in the spring I started vending these products directly to the public through two north Whidbey farmers' markets. Having served many happy taste buds and made great strides with the company, at the end of the first year I decided to take my company in a new direction, and on March 29, 2016, I made my last WIBC cookie delivery.

More than one year in the making, this book marks the pivot of my company's focus onto what I enjoy most about baking – creating recipes that I have imagined and sharing the results with friends, inspiring others in baking, and connecting people through good food.

Inside you will find over 50 proven recipes including the Whidbey Island Baking Company commercially-baked goods and special-order cookies; there are also some coffee and family recipes, and a few delicious main courses. I believe that bakers and cooks of all skill levels will find these recipes accessible and engaging. When prepared correctly, these recipes will produce tasty results and, in most cases, are healthier approaches to cookies and other baked goods.

Many of my recipes have their own stories – usually having to do with the person I developed the concoction with or who I made it for. My stories are at the beginning of their recipes – as you prepare and serve these, I am sure you will start to find your own stories. Some of my recipes feature ways to produce alternative flavours – which are in the Tips & Thoughts at the end of the recipes or close of the chapters. I aim to inspire – as you make the cookies in the following pages, you may begin to see where to make modifications and develop the baked items that you imagine – and when you do, I would be pleased if you would message me.

~

Before starting Whidbey Island Baking Company, I had been training for a career change while supporting myself as a 'starving artist' playing Highland bagpipes. Money was tight, and Christmases proved to be tricky. Being resourceful, I found I could participate in gift giving by preparing baked goods. For a week I would labour in my kitchen, load my mountain bike with bags of cookies, and trek around to my friends' houses in the cold and wet Puget Sound weather. It became common during these visits that my friends would suggest that I go into the baking business. When I made my 2012 cookie delivery to my friend Rene and her family, I received the same urging – the difference being that Rene related her experiences establishing three small businesses (yes, *three*) to how I might build a baking company of my own. Since then she has provided further encouragement and gave me the idea of writing a recipe book – *this book!* Her vision and inspiration have gone a long way – and I'm not done yet – *Thanks, Rene!*

I grew up half in Seattle and half on Whidbey Island, and when I moved to the island – or what we affectionately refer to as "The Rock" – full-time it was in large part to start Whidbey Island Baking Company. A few months following, I attended a workshop on self-publishing at my local library presented by Tom Trimbath. Over the course of the evening, I found his delivery to be down-to-earth, focused, and imbued with his natural humor. I have since attended other book presentations by Tom and frequently run into him – he is always a good soul to connect with. When I conceived the idea of changing WIBC from production baking to writing recipe books, Tom was – of course –the first person I called. He has been of consummate support of my endeavour and helped to walk me through the process. *Thanks, Tom!*

You will – of course – notice images of Whidbey Island and its wildlife featured in this book. These were taken by Cara Lynnae Hefflinger, whom I was familiar with for a year or two before I learned she was a photographer. Then and now, whenever I see her pictures my jaw drops. When she gave her very kind permission for me to use a selection of her work I was overjoyed! I knew that her photographs would show the beauty of the island that is appreciated by everyone who lives here. If you ever get to meet Cara, be prepared to be wowed by her photography and to pass out laughing because of her rapid wit. *Thanks, Cara!*

My mom was one of the first of all the people I spoke with when I began thinking about starting Whidbey Island Baking Company. Imagine telling your parents that you are considering switching from being a "Professional Starving Artist" to a "Small Business Owner Building A Company From The Ground Up On A Shoestring Budget" – it can be like saying that you are going on tour with a band or joining the circus. I made my pitch, and my mom has been nothing but supportive ever since. When I was unavailable to vend at my own farmers market booth, she filled in with my dad. She opened the door for WIBC to vend at quilt shows along with promoting my upcoming recipe book as soon as this project got underway. She contributed both baking recipes from when WIBC was in production and family recipes for this book. She doesn't quit – *Thanks, Mom!*

For the innumerable hours I spent working to launch Whidbey Island Baking Company, making and packaging cookies in the bakery to setting up and vending at farmers' markets, my dad spent at least half as many hours and probably more supporting my endeavour. He made most of the WIBC deliveries, promoted my business and products in his own time, calmly listened when I dealt with the growing pains of a small business, prepared meals when I put in long and late hours, listened to my ideas and gave encouragement as I worked to write this book. I am forever grateful for his help, and the time I got to spend with him working on this labor of love. *Thanks, Dad!*

Twice I have received support from The British Isles. A few weeks before opening Whidbey Island Baking Company I asked for some assistance from my bagpiper friend Donna in Scotland. Donna previously brought various bagpipe related websites to fruition for me – this time she helped walk me through everything I needed to know how to build and launch WhidbeyIslandBaking.com. During the last weeks of finishing this book, I went to social media, posting progress updates for the pending publication. Seeing a need for some editing help, Katie in England, contacted me and volunteered. The recipes that follow are presented in both U.S. Standard & Metric, and Katie double checked my conversions. Donna and Katie both helped me further in identifying the differences of ingredient names. *Cheers, Donna and Katie!*

Since the inception of Whidbey Island Baking Company and this recipe book project I have received an outpour of support from friends – at home, across the country, and abroad. As I transitioned out of production and into writing, Von, an established author in Washington State, helped explain aspects of the literary industry. Eryn, from Montana, sent recipes for my coffee section and provided photos. Arne & Chris in New York have been consummate supporters. Adam, one of the most brilliant and creative artists I know, crafted my company logo. Victoria, a bagpiper friend and company owner in British Columbia, Canada, gave me small business consultation and even helped get marketing supplies for WIBC. There are just too many great folks to name – so if you think I'm talking about you, then you're probably right. And all I can do is keep saying thank you, Thank You, *Thank You!*

Now, without further delay – Please, *Enjoy!*

Slàinte Mhath, (Good Health)

Don P. Scoby
December 1, 2016

PS – *Hi Mom & Dad!*

~

Addendum – August 31, 2018

About a year and eight months ago I was close to publishing this book when my hard drive **CRASHED**. I had previously developed the attitude of *"That will never happen to me!"* and at best I only occasionally made back-ups. Trying to see if my data could be saved I checked with my experts. Two generous gents – Jim in Mount Vernon and George in Shoreline, Washington – did everything in their vast knowledge to recover my data. I sent my hard drive off to a few labs for possible data retrieval, and in the end nothing could be recovered. In the mean time George rebuilt my laptop for me and even gave me a bigger and better hard drive from his personal supply. A few weeks later I got lucky and found a back-up of my manuscript that was a number of months old – *which I didn't remember making!* The bulk of my work was intact along with recipes I had otherwise lost and I was able to restart this project. I learned a hard lesson – *BACK UP YOUR HARD DRIVE*. When things looked bleak two men stepped up, offered their time and help, and gave me hope – *Thank you, Jim and George!*

After my project got back underway in June 2017 I was contacted online by Linda Luhman offering her proofreading and editorial skills. The following autumn I got to meet Linda while I was in Minnesota – I was in Hastings to play my friends' wedding and she was nearby on vacation. What was projected to be a causal one hour business meeting in a local restaurant turned into hours of laughter, stories, and ... oh yeah, talking about her editing my book. I easily became convinced about her abilities and that she would make the process fun. By the time I got back from Minnesota Linda had already dove into the work with vigor; she presented sharp and creative suggestions that were well supported. With Linda's help, my book became a better crafted project and a stronger creation than I previously imagined or achieved on my own. She is also the artist behind the Bigfoot and Chupacabra cartoons featured with my two Monster Cookie recipes. *Thanks, Linda!*

During the first year of working on this book I thought to test my writing, which I finally got to try during August and September of 2017. I asked online for volunteers from people who followed my company. I sought individuals who varied in skill, ranging from novices to experienced bakers. These *Test Bakers* received a small number of my biscotti and Cookie Square recipes to experiment with and give me feedback on my writing and their baking experience. Not only did everyone do well, they pointed out details I could clarify and suggested ideas I had not thought of. The bakers who completed the project received their pick of one of my recipes before my book was released. This proved to be fun for everyone involved and I would like to repeat the experiment with future books. For me it was invaluable, and *each of my Test Bakers have my Thanks* – Arne and Chris in New York, Catherine in Minnesota, CJ here in Washington State, Deb right here on Whidbey Island, and Linda in Wisconsin.

In the fall of 2017 I started thinking about releasing this book in e-reader format following paper publication. After making a few comments online, Aleta contacted me from Texas. She pointed out that I would need an e-reader throughout the process to make sure my book was converting correctly, and asked if I had one. I did not, and Aleta kindly sent me one from her collection. As soon as I can I will make my book available as an e-book – and Aleta helped to make that happen. *Thanks, Aleta!*

For me food is about joy, health, and people connecting with people. At my request, a select group of unique individuals have helped to bring this out in my book better than I ever possibly could have alone. Friends from all over – and even my own mom – appear as guest writers, contributing *wonderful* opening introductions to each chapter. *With my gratitude*, please enjoy the writings from...

Philomina, now here in Washington State ~ Cookie Squares
Giovanna in Georgia ~ Biscotti
Lynn on Whidbey Island ~ More Cookies
Colleen in Michigan ~ Coffee, Coffee Cake, and Applesauce
...and...
Arne in New York ~ Main Courses

Finally, my thanks to two top-notch photographers whose contributions came during the last weeks of this project ... At the end of the first two chapters you will find photos that demonstrate how to prepare my cookie squares and biscotti. These series of photo were taken by Brian Smith, whom I had the pleasure of getting to work with serving as my own hand-model. When we were finished with these pictures, Brian looked at me with a spark and said, *"Now I'm going to get creative!"* He proceeded to arrange my cookies along with the other baking props I had brought and took striking photos – a few of these are at the beginning of these chapters. The pictures Brian captured are greater than anything I had ever imagined possible for my book. In 2013 I was a featured musician on Geoff Castle's Celtic Christmas tour. The tour remains as one of the greatest music experiences I have had to date. Every show Geoff and his band put on was big, and the two we played in Anacortes, WA, were *HUGE!* Unbeknownst to me, Chris Terrell was taking photos throughout the shows, and during the high-energy final number of the night he took a photo of me that has become one of my favourite performance pictures. When I contacted him to request if I could use it in my book, he neither said yes or no, instead he saw that my needs were taken care of by asking if I had a high enough fidelity picture. Brian, Chris – *gentlemen, Thank You!*

MEASUREMENT CONVERSIONS & INGREDIENT NAMES

The measurements in this book are provided in both U.S. Standard & Metric. Weights, measurements, and dimensions have been converted. Temperatures are in Fahrenheit, Celsius, and Gas Mark. All conversions are listed side by side – *for example* – 2 cups/480 ml, 1 inch/2.5 centimeters, and 325° F/165° C/Gas Mark 3.

Shortly after starting work on this book, it was suggested that I provide these conversions as opposed to *only* presenting my measurements in U.S. Standard and Fahrenheit. Performing these calculations once is more efficient than it would be by everyone who prefers to work in metric – and it makes my book ready to be enjoyed in all regions from the moment of publication. To me this is an idea that simply makes good sense, and it is my intention to do this with all future books.

Please also note that my recipes only list the general names of ingredients as used in the U.S. These variations should be as follows:

Baking Soda / Bicarbonate of Soda
All-Purpose flour / Plain flour

As you use this book if you find ingredients that need to be clarified, please contact me. If necessary, we will get these figured out – and I can add them above in following editions.

COOKIE SQUARES

| Almond Cranberry | Brunetties | Butterscotch Blondie Coffee | Chocolate Peppermint | Cranberry Orange | Dirty Blondies | Chocolate Chip | Double Chocolate | Espresso Chocolate Chip | Lemon | Mint Chocolate Chip | Strawberry Lemonade | Chocolate Citrus | Chocolate Raspberry | Lemon Citrus | Lemon Lime | Lemon Raspberry |

JOURNEY

One of my college professors taught that sharing food is one of the most basic ways people show love and care for one another. Baking especially has always been an activity that I've enjoyed with my nearest and dearest.

Some of my favorite memories are of time with my best friend in her kitchen during our annual Christmas cookie marathon baking sessions. We spent many years bouncing ideas off each other, discussing different flavor combinations, and perfecting our own special cookie recipes.

Life has since taken me a couple of time zones away from my best friend's kitchen, however; it has led to the opportunity to meet new friends to bake with, such as the author of this book. It's been a great joy for me getting to know Don and making all sorts of treats with him.

I hope you find some recipes here that you can share with loved ones and make some memories of your own.

Philomina ~ Washington, USA

ALMOND CRANBERRY COOKIE SQUARES

Soon after developing my first WIBC Cookie Square products I became tempted by the idea of making an almond version. Although I knew to base it off of my Toasted Almond Biscotti, the cookie in my mind lacked something. This changed around mid-June 2016 when I had the opportunity to see Ellen – a friend through the Scottish community who I had not seen in a few years and was an early supporter of my baking business. I wanted to bring some cookies to show what I had accomplished with my company, so I found out her favourite flavours. This launched an experiment – to make a batch of Almond Cranberry Biscotti! When I ran short on time preparing for the visit, I realized two things ... I could make a round of Cookie Squares faster than biscotti, and dried cranberries were EXACTLY the inspiration that my Almond Cookie Squares had been looking for. On my first attempt, the recipe was a hit – this one is for you, Ellen!

U.S. STANDARD – METRIC	INGREDIENT
12 Tablespoons – 180 ml	Unsalted Butter, softened
1 1/2 cup – 360 ml	White Sugar
2	Large Eggs
4 Tablespoons – 60 ml	Water
4 teaspoons – 20 ml	Pure Almond Extract
4 teaspoons – 20 ml	Pure Vanilla Extract
1 1/2 teaspoons – 7.5 ml	Baking Powder
2 1/3 cups – 560 ml	All-Purpose Flour
1 cups – 240 ml	Sliced Almonds
1 cups – 240 ml	Dried Cranberries

MIXING
1. In a mixing bowl, cream butter and then combine the sugar. It may be necessary to stop mixing and scrape the bottom of the bowl so that butter and sugar are mixed uniformly.
2. Beat in eggs, water, almond and vanilla extracts and baking powder.
3. While mixing, add one cup of flour at a time. Avoid over-mixing the flour; if necessary, stop mixing between making measurements and adding flour.

4. Add the sliced almonds and dried cranberries as the last of the flour becomes completely blended.

BAKING
1. Heat oven to 325° F/165° C/Gas Mark 3.
2. Using cooking spray or lining with parchment paper, prepare a 9 x 13 inch baking pan. Transfer the dough from mixing the bowl to the center of your pan and spread evenly.
3. Place pan in the middle of the oven and bake for 45 minutes.
4. When a knife blade or toothpick comes out clean, remove pan from oven and set on a cooling rack.
5. Once completely cooled, cut into 32 even pieces. This may be done in the pan. Alternatively, the entire non-cut baked good can be removed from the pan and cut on a cutting board. Store in a tightly sealed container.

TIPS & THOUGHTS
In place of the dried cranberries, I encourage you to experiment with other dried fruits and berries. Apples, apricots, açaí, or blackberries – use your imagination and let me know how it goes! Hmm... almond and candied-ginger?

PAIRINGS
Experiment – let me know what you think!

BRUNETTIE COOKIE SQUARES
Well, you've heard of Blondies, right?
These are better.

I tried a few new things around the time I made my Butterscotch Blondie Coffee Cookie Squares. Trying to make a darker and chewier cookie, I used only brown sugar and switched the vanilla extract with dark molasses. The first batch must have turned out good because people made them disappear. With their rich color and distinct flavour it only made sense to call them Brunetties.

U.S. STANDARD – METRIC	INGREDIENT
12 Tablespoons – 180 ml	Unsalted Butter, softened
1 1/2 cup – 360 ml	Brown Sugar
2	Large Eggs
5 Tablespoons – 75 ml	Strong Coffee or Espresso
2 teaspoons – 10 ml	Pure Vanilla Extract
2 Tablespoons – 30 ml	Dark Molasses
1 1/2 teaspoons – 7.5 ml	Baking Powder
2 1/3 cups – 560 ml	All-Purpose Flour
2 cups – 480 ml	Semi-Sweet Chocolate Chips

MIXING
1. In a mixing bowl, cream butter and then combine the sugar. It may be necessary to stop mixing and scrape the bottom of the bowl so that butter and sugar are mixed uniformly.
2. Beat in eggs, coffee or espresso, and vanilla extract. Follow with the measure of baking powder.
3. While mixing, add one cup of flour at a time. Avoid over-mixing the flour; if necessary, stop mixing between making measurements and adding flour.
4. Add the chocolate chips as the last of the flour becomes completely blended.

BAKING
1. Heat oven to 325° F/165° C/Gas Mark 3.
2. Using cooking spray or lining with parchment paper, prepare a 9 x 13 inch baking pan. Transfer the dough from mixing the bowl to the center of your pan and spread evenly.
3. Place pan in the middle of the oven and bake for 45 minutes.
4. When a knife blade or toothpick comes out clean, remove pan from oven and set on a cooling rack.
5. Once completely cooled, cut into 32 even pieces. This may be done in the pan. Alternatively, the entire non-cut baked good can be removed from the pan and cut on a cutting board. Store in a tightly sealed container.

BUTTERSCOTCH BLONDIE COFFEE COOKIE SQUARES

While this name is long – which is fun in and of itself – if I am not mistaken a 'Blondie' is the plain dough part of the cookie. So, truth and accuracy in my titling, I believe having 'butterscotch' in the name not only sounds more enticing but also speaks to the embellishments.

Once you make these Butterscotch Blondie Coffee Cookie Squares, you are going to have to decide if you hide and keep them to yourself, share only with people you like, or share a little with people you do not like so that you may manipulate them to your will ... which, with these, ought to be easy.

U.S. STANDARD – METRIC	INGREDIENT
12 Tablespoons – 180 ml	Unsalted Butter, softened
3/4 cup – 180 ml	White Sugar
3/4 cup – 180 ml	Brown Sugar
2	Large Eggs
5 Tablespoons – 75 ml	Strong Coffee or Espresso
2 teaspoons – 10 ml	Pure Vanilla Extract
1 1/2 teaspoons – 7.5 ml	Baking Powder
2 1/3 cups – 560 ml	All-Purpose Flour

2 cups – 480 ml..Butterscotch Chips

MIXING
1. In a mixing bowl, cream butter and then combine the sugar. It may be necessary to stop mixing and scrape the bottom of the bowl so that butter and sugar are mixed uniformly.
2. Beat in eggs, coffee or espresso, and vanilla extract. Follow with the measure of baking powder.
3. While mixing, add one cup of flour at a time. Avoid over-mixing the flour; if necessary, stop mixing between making measurements and adding flour.
4. Add the butterscotch chips as the last of the flour becomes completely blended.

BAKING
1. Heat oven to 325° F/165° C/Gas Mark 3.
2. Using cooking spray or lining with parchment paper, prepare a 9 x 13 inch baking pan. Transfer the dough from mixing the bowl to the center of your pan and spread evenly.
3. Place pan in the middle of the oven and bake for 45 minutes.
4. When a knife blade or toothpick comes out clean, remove pan from oven and set on a cooling rack.
5. Once completely cooled, cut into 32 even pieces. This may be done in the pan. Alternatively, the entire non-cut baked good can be removed from the pan and cut on a cutting board. Store in a tightly sealed container.

TIPS & THOUGHTS
I first made some Butterscotch Blondies using left-over butterscotch chips from baking with my friend, Philomina (and so he doesn't feel left out, *JR was there at the time*). The recipe I used was simple and tasty, but – as I often find – it had too much butter in it and came out greasy. So of course, I think two things – how to make it as a Cookie Square, and how to make a better cookie that is not greasy. When Phil (*and JR*) was visiting, she also made some cookies using butterscotch pudding. So I thought that including aspects of these pudding cookies could both bring in more flavour and the needed moisture when I reduced the butter.

My first attempt at these Cookie Squares came after thinking about how to do the recipe for two weeks. Of course, I didn't just sit around all that time like the Thinking Man statue contemplating this recipe – I allowed these to ruminate in the back of my mind – and two weeks is relatively short. I've let recipes bounce around in my head for as much as three months before I get the "Aha!" and try it ... but usually that's when I nail the recipe, and it comes out great the first time.

I realized that with this I ought to try the simple, obvious approach first. I was hung up on the 5 tablespoons of liquid when I decided just to try coffee. I also opted to go with (approximately) half butterscotch chips and half white chips. My original plan was to use all butterscotch chips, but the bag of butterscotch chips I got was under 2 cups, so I was going to have to make up the difference anyway. So, I thought, why not go half and half butterscotch and white chips so I could make a second experimental batch – besides, the butterscotch flavour mostly comes from the brown sugar in the dough anyway.

Fascinating? Maybe not ... but that's how my recipe thought process tends to work. And to think that people say I need to get out more?!?

CHOCOLATE PEPPERMINT COOKIE SQUARES
One word ...

YUM!

U.S. STANDARD – METRIC	INGREDIENT
12 Tablespoons – 180 ml	Unsalted Butter, softened
1 1/2 cup – 360 ml	White Sugar
2	Large Eggs
5 Tablespoon – 75 ml	Strong Coffee or Espresso
2 teaspoons – 10 ml	Pure Peppermint Extract
1 1/2 teaspoons – 7.5 ml	Baking Powder
1/3 cup – 80 ml	Unsweetened Cocoa Powder
2 cups – 480 ml	All-Purpose Flour
2 cups – 480 ml	White Chocolate Chips

MIXING
1. In a mixing bowl, cream butter and then combine the sugar. It may be necessary to stop mixing and scrape the bottom of bowl so that butter and sugar are mixed uniformly.

2. Beat in eggs, coffee, and extract. Followed by mixing in baking powder and cocoa powder.
3. While mixing, add one cup of flour at a time. Avoid over-mixing the flour; if necessary, stop mixing between making measurements and adding flour.
4. Add the chocolate chips as the last of the flour becomes completely blended.

BAKING
1. Heat oven to 325° F/165° C/Gas Mark 3.
2. Using cooking spray or lining with parchment paper, prepare a 9 x 13 inch baking pan. Transfer the dough from mixing the bowl to the center of your pan and spread evenly.
3. Place pan in the middle of the oven and bake for 45 minutes.
4. When a knife blade or toothpick comes out clean, remove pan from oven and set on a cooling rack.
5. Once completely cooled, cut into 32 even pieces. This may be done in the pan. Alternatively, the entire non-cut baked good can be removed from the pan and cut on a cutting board. Store in a tightly sealed container.

TIPS & THOUGHTS
I recommend making the Chocolate Peppermint, Chocolate Orange, or Chocolate Raspberry versions with white chocolate chips. These help to differentiate their appearance from the Double Chocolate Cookie Squares. White chocolate chips tend to be more expensive than regular chocolate chips; for this reason, and for a stronger chocolate flavour presence, you may prefer to make these recipes with chocolate chips.

PAIRINGS
Coffee, hot chocolate ... these are so good you'll just want to eat them as they are!

CRANBERRY ORANGE COOKIE SQUARES

I tend to think of my Cookie Square recipes as being pretty casual cookies – 'comfort food' some might say. The Cranberry Orange and the Almond Cranberry Cookie Squares, however, seem to make something a little more ... sophisticated.

U.S. STANDARD – METRIC	INGREDIENT
12 Tablespoons – 180 ml	Unsalted Butter, softened
1 1/2 cup – 360 ml	White Sugar
2	Large Eggs
5 Tablespoons – 75 ml	Orange Juice
2 teaspoons – 10 ml	Pure Orange Extract
3-4 drops	Yellow Food Colouring
3-4 drops	Red Food Colouring
1 1/2 teaspoons – 7.5 ml	Baking Powder
2 1/3 cups – 560 ml	All-Purpose Flour
2 cups – 480 ml	Dried Cranberries

MIXING

1. In a mixing bowl, cream butter and then combine the sugar. It may be necessary to stop mixing and scrape the bottom of the bowl so that butter and sugar are mixed uniformly.
2. Beat in eggs, orange juice, and extract. Follow with yellow and red food colouring and baking powder.
3. While mixing, add one cup of flour at a time. Avoid over-mixing the flour; if necessary, stop mixing between making measurements and adding flour.
4. Add the dried cranberries as the last of the flour becomes completely blended.

BAKING

1. Heat oven to 325° F/165° C/Gas Mark 3.
2. Using cooking spray or lining with parchment paper, prepare a 9 x 13 inch baking pan. Transfer the dough from mixing the bowl to the center of your pan and spread evenly.
3. Place pan in the middle of the oven and bake for 45 minutes.

4. When a knife blade or toothpick comes out clean, remove pan from oven and set on a cooling rack.
5. Once completely cooled, cut into 32 even pieces. This may be done in the pan. Alternatively, the entire non-cut baked good can be removed from the pan and cut on a cutting board. Store in a tightly sealed container.

TIPS & THOUGHTS

While bottled orange juice is perfectly acceptable with this recipe, fresh is always best. It takes a little work to juice an orange half, but it adds to the accomplishment and usually makes for a wonderful smell.

PAIRINGS

Tea and a nice afternoon chat with friends. While I prefer herbal teas, I imagine these Cranberry-Orange Cookie Squares going especially well with various kinds of black tea.

DIRTY BLONDIE COOKIE SQUARES
OR
CHOCOLATE CHIP COOKIE SQUARES

These are the cookies I've been looking for!

When first attempting to develop the WIBC Cookie Square product line I began by making Chocolate Chip Cookie Squares. What came out was dissatisfying – the cookies either had too much butter or they were too dry. Two years after starting this book, while trying to create my Brunetties recipe, I accidently made and perfected the Chocolate Chip Cookie Squares ... YAY! I also call them Dirty Blondie Cookie Squares – *it's more fun*.

U.S. STANDARD – METRIC	INGREDIENT
12 Tablespoons – 180 ml	Unsalted Butter, softened
3/4 cup – 180 ml	White Sugar
3/4 cup – 180 ml	Brown Sugar
2	Large Eggs
5 Tablespoons – 75 ml	Strong Coffee or Espresso
2 teaspoons – 10 ml	Pure Vanilla Extract
1 1/2 teaspoons – 7.5 ml	Baking Powder
2 1/3 cups – 560 ml	All-Purpose Flour
2 cups – 480 ml	Semi-Sweet Chocolate Chips

MIXING

1. In a mixing bowl, cream butter and then combine the sugar. It may be necessary to stop mixing and scrape the bottom of the bowl so that butter and sugar are mixed uniformly.
2. Beat in eggs, coffee or espresso, and vanilla extract. Follow with the measure of baking powder.
3. While mixing, add one cup of flour at a time. Avoid overmixing the flour; if necessary, stop mixing between making measurements and adding flour.
4. Add the chocolate chips as the last of the flour becomes completely blended.

BAKING
1. Heat oven to 325° F/165° C/Gas Mark 3.
2. Using cooking spray or lining with parchment paper, prepare a 9 x 13 inch baking pan. Transfer the dough from mixing the bowl to the center of your pan and spread evenly.
3. Place pan in the middle of the oven and bake for 45 minutes.
4. When a knife blade or toothpick comes out clean, remove pan from oven and set on a cooling rack.
5. Once completely cooled, cut into 32 even pieces. This may be done in the pan. Alternatively, the entire non-cut baked good can be removed from the pan and cut on a cutting board. Store in a tightly sealed container.

TIPS & THOUGHTS
The easiest and most obvious tweak to this recipe would be to add some crushed walnuts. Peanuts would be another good choice. For a fun visual flair, replace half or the whole measure of chocolate chips with the "Popular Colorful Candy Coated Chocolates" I eluded to in my Original Bigfoot Monster Cookies recipe.

PAIRINGS
With this classic cookie flavour, the obvious pairing is milk and kids! I would also dunk this in my coffee, pack this along a hike or picnic, or make this very easy cookie and share it at work.

DOUBLE CHOCOLATE COOKIE SQUARES

When I make these Double Chocolate Cookie Squares some people think I've baked brownies with chocolate chips. Apparently they *really like* my "chocolate chip brownies", and then all of my cookies disappear. What's in a name – if they're happy, I'm happy – so I've stopped clarifying that these are cookies.

Please ... enjoy the Chocolate Chip Brownie Cookies.

U.S. STANDARD – METRIC	INGREDIENT
12 Tablespoons – 180 ml	Unsalted Butter, softened
1 1/2 cup – 360 ml	White Sugar
2	Large Eggs
5 Tablespoon – 75 ml	Strong Coffee or Espresso
2 teaspoon – 10 ml	Pure Vanilla Extract
1 1/2 teaspoons – 7.5 ml	Baking Powder
1/3 cup – 80 ml	Unsweetened Cocoa Powder
2 cups – 480 ml	All-Purpose Flour
2 cups – 480 ml	Semi-Sweet Chocolate Chips

MIXING
1. In a mixing bowl, cream butter and then combine the sugar. It may be necessary to stop mixing and scrape the bottom of the bowl so that butter and sugar are mixed uniformly.
2. Beat in eggs, coffee, and extract followed by baking powder and cocoa powder.
3. While mixing, add one cup of flour at a time. Avoid over-mixing the flour; if necessary, stop mixing between making measurements and adding flour.
4. Add the chocolate chips as the last of the flour becomes completely blended.

BAKING
1. Heat oven to 325° F/165° C/Gas Mark 3.
2. Using cooking spray or lining with parchment paper, prepare a 9 x 13 inch baking pan. Transfer the dough from mixing the bowl to the center of your pan and spread evenly.
3. Place pan in the middle of the oven and bake for 45 minutes.
4. When a knife blade or toothpick comes out clean, remove pan from oven and set on a cooling rack.
5. Once completely cooled, cut into 32 even pieces. This may be done in the pan. Alternatively, the entire non-cut baked good can be removed from the pan and cut on a cutting board. Store in a tightly sealed container.

TIPS & THOUGHTS
For some reason, when I created this recipe it came out more moist than my Chocolate Peppermint Cookie Squares – so this may take some experimenting to perfect it – try playing around with the bake time and temperature, possibly add a few teaspoons of butter.

Switching out the chocolate chips for various dried berries could produce additional pleasing combinations – cranberries, blueberries, raspberries, açaí berries – the options are as wide as your creativity and experimentation. Candied ginger could also be a tasty option.

PAIRINGS
Pretty much EVERYTHING!

ESPRESSO CHOCOLATE CHIP COOKIE SQUARES

My Espresso Chocolate Chip and Lemon Cookie Squares were the first two WIBC Cookie Square products – both of which my customers gave an immediate and strong positive response to. With the popularity of coffee, watch your friends and family members when you serve these ... I'm betting you will receive a similar reaction. *Enjoy!*

U.S. STANDARD – METRIC	INGREDIENT
16 Tablespoons – 240 ml	Unsalted Butter, softened
3/4 cup – 180 ml	White Sugar
3/4 cup – 180 ml	Brown Sugar, packed
2	Large Eggs
5 Tablespoon – 75 ml	Strong Coffee or Espresso
2 teaspoon – 10 ml	Pure Vanilla Extract
3 Tablespoon – 45 ml	Coffee, ground
1 1/2 teaspoons – 7.5 ml	Baking Powder
2 cups – 480 ml	All-Purpose Flour
2 cups – 480 ml	Semi-Sweet Chocolate Chips

MIXING
1. In a mixing bowl, cream butter and then combine the sugar. It may be necessary to stop mixing and scrape the bottom of the bowl so that butter and sugar are mixed uniformly.
2. Beat in eggs, coffee, and extract followed by baking powder and ground coffee.
3. While mixing, add one cup of flour at a time. Avoid over-mixing the flour; if necessary, stop mixing between making measurements and adding flour.
4. Add the chocolate chips as the last of the flour becomes completely blended.

BAKING
1. Heat oven to 325° F/165° C/Gas Mark 3.
2. Using cooking spray or lining with parchment paper, prepare a 9 x 13 inch baking pan. Transfer the dough from mixing the bowl to the center of your pan and spread evenly.
3. Place pan in the middle of the oven and bake for 45 minutes.
4. When a knife blade or toothpick comes out clean, remove pan from oven and set on a cooling rack.
5. Once completely cooled, cut into 32 even pieces. This may be done in the pan. Alternatively, the entire non-cut baked good can be removed from the pan and cut on a cutting board. Store in a tightly sealed container.

TIPS & THOUGHTS
Some people dislike the texture of the ground coffee. I have made this recipe substituting the 3 Tablespoons ground coffee for 2 Tablespoons mocha paste. In my opinion, this recipe was even better with the mocha paste, and I planned to re-release the product on the market as Mocha Chocolate Chip Cookie Squares.

PAIRINGS
Classic – milk and cookies!

LEMON COOKIE SQUARES
If you like lemon, you are going to LOVE these!

Here is how good these cookies are ...
The WIBC Lemon Cookie Squares made their debut at the Oak Harbor farmers market during the summer of 2015. A family came into my tent and bought a number of cookies, and among their selection was this brand-new product. Only minutes after leaving my tent, their son returned to buy another package of my Lemon Cookie Squares. Never saying a word, he made his selection and purchase with one hand while polishing off the first cookie with his other hand.
There are funny little compliments that occur when you properly prepare a good recipe like this one – *and I'll take them!* I hope you have as much fun presenting these Lemon Cookie Squares as I do.

U.S. STANDARD – METRIC	INGREDIENT
12 Tablespoons – 180 ml	Unsalted Butter, softened
1 1/2 cup – 360 ml	White Sugar
2	Large Eggs
5 Tablespoons – 75 ml	Lemon Juice
2 teaspoons – 10 ml	Pure Lemon Extract
5 drops	Yellow Food Colouring
1 1/2 teaspoons – 7.5 ml	Baking Powder
2 1/3 cups – 560 ml	All-Purpose Flour
2 cups – 480 ml	White Chocolate Chips

MIXING
1. In a mixing bowl, cream butter and then combine the sugar. It may be necessary to stop mixing and scrape the bottom of the bowl so that butter and sugar are mixed uniformly.
2. Beat in eggs, lemon juice, and lemon extract. Follow with yellow food colouring and baking powder.
3. While mixing, add one cup of flour at a time. Avoid overmixing the flour; if necessary, stop mixing between making measurements and adding flour.
4. Add the white chocolate chips as the last of the flour becomes completely blended.

BAKING
1. Heat oven to 325° F/165° C/Gas Mark 3.
2. Using cooking spray or lining with parchment paper, prepare a 9 x 13 inch baking pan. Transfer the dough from mixing the bowl to the center of your pan and spread evenly.
3. Place pan in the middle of the oven and bake for 45 minutes.
4. When a knife blade or toothpick comes out clean, remove pan from oven and set on a cooling rack.
5. Once completely cooled, cut into 32 even pieces. This may be done in the pan. Alternatively, the entire non-cut baked good can be removed from the pan and cut on a cutting board. Store in a tightly sealed container.

TIPS & THOUGHTS
There are a few options I have tried when making my Lemon Cookie Squares. Simply follow the recipe as directed and switch 1 cup of the white chocolate chips for chopped candied ginger, dried cranberries, or dried blueberries for pleasing variations.

The first time my friends JR & Philomina visited me on the island, Phil requested that I make my Lemon Cookie Squares with some wild blackberries that grew nearby. The cookies that came out of my oven tasted as fantastic as they looked and smelled, and it was fun to make her idea into a reality. To do this in your kitchen substitute 1 cup of the white chocolate chips for frozen berries and add about 10 minutes to your bake time.

PAIRINGS
You can pretty much never go wrong with good ol' milk and cookies. In particular, I like sweet vanilla almond milk with these.

Lemon Cookie Squares with Whidbey Island wild blackberries.

MINT CHOCOLATE CHIP COOKIE SQUARES
What follows was a very successful experiMINT...

While finishing this book, I found a recipe online for Mint Chocolate Chip Cookies ... and got *inspired!*

U.S. STANDARD – METRIC	INGREDIENT
12 Tablespoons – 180 ml	Unsalted Butter, softened
1 1/2 cup – 360 ml	White Sugar
2	Large Eggs
2 teaspoons – 10 ml (or more to taste)	Pure Peppermint Extract
5 Tablespoons – 75 ml	Water
10 drops (no, really)	Green Food Colouring
1 1/2 teaspoons – 7.5 ml	Baking Powder
2 1/3 cups – 560 ml	All-Purpose Flour
2 cups – 480 ml	Semi-Sweet Chocolate Chips

MIXING
1. In a mixing bowl, cream butter and then combine the sugar. It may be necessary to stop mixing and scrape the bottom of the bowl so that butter and sugar are mixed uniformly.
2. Beat in eggs, water, and peppermint extract. Follow with green food colouring and baking powder.
3. While mixing, add one cup of flour at a time. Avoid over-mixing the flour; if necessary, stop mixing between making measurements and adding flour.
4. Add the chocolate chips as the last of the flour becomes completely blended.

BAKING
1. Heat oven to 325° F/165° C/Gas Mark 3.
2. Using cooking spray or lining with parchment paper, prepare a 9 x 13 inch baking pan. Transfer the dough from mixing the bowl to the center of your pan and spread evenly.
3. Place pan in the middle of the oven and bake for 45 minutes.
4. When a knife blade or toothpick comes out clean, remove pan from oven and set on a cooling rack.
5. Once completely cooled, cut into 32 even pieces. This may be done in the pan. Alternatively, the entire non-cut baked good can be removed from the pan and cut on a cutting board. Store in a tightly sealed container.

TIPS & THOUGHTS

Some bakers dust their chocolate chips with flour before mixing them into their cookie dough – this is supposed to keep the chips from sticking together and disperse better throughout the dough.

After the first time that I made these I thought, "What if I put in *MORE* chocolate chips?" Something about that still seems ... *enticing*.

PAIRINGS

I dipped these in coffee and enjoyed it – but then I dunk all my cookies in my coffee if I have some. Experiment and let me know what combinations you find pleasing. I imagine that kids and milk would be perfect, and as well that there are some blends with tea that would be exquisite.

If you have the right cookie that is soft enough to break with a utensil – like many of these Cookie Square recipes – put one in a bowl with ice cream ... I would not blame you if you put in two! Chocolate ice cream, vanilla ice cream ... some of each ...

STRAWBERRY LEMONADE COOKIE SQUARES
These taste like summer.

U.S. STANDARD – METRIC | INGREDIENT

U.S. STANDARD – METRIC	INGREDIENT
12 Tablespoons – 180 ml	Unsalted Butter, softened
1 1/2 cup – 360 ml	White Sugar
2	Large Eggs
5 Tablespoons – 75 ml	Lemon Juice
2 teaspoons – 10 ml	Pure Lemon Extract
5 drops	Yellow Food Colouring
1 1/2 teaspoons – 7.5 ml	Baking Powder
2 1/3 cups – 560 ml	All-Purpose Flour
1 cup – 240 ml	White Chocolate Chips
1 cup – 240 ml	Strawberries

STRAWBERRY PREPARATION

If using fresh strawberries, carefully cut your berries on a cutting board with a sharp knife into 1/4 to 1/2 inch/6 to 12 millimeter pieces and freeze. If using frozen strawberries you may find that you prefer to use a serrated knife. In the event these frozen strawberries thaw while cutting, return them to your freezer to harden again. These need to be frozen and added late when they go in the dough to keep from disintegrating as they mix in.

MIXING
1. In a mixing bowl, cream butter and then combine the sugar. It may be necessary to stop mixing and scrape the bottom of the bowl so that butter and sugar are mixed uniformly.
2. Beat in eggs, lemon juice, and lemon extract. Follow with yellow food colouring and baking powder.
3. While mixing, add one cup of flour at a time. Avoid over-mixing the flour; if necessary, stop mixing between making measurements and adding flour.
4. Add the white chocolate chips and frozen strawberries as the last of the flour becomes completely blended. You may find you prefer to do this by hand.

BAKING
1. Heat oven to 325° F/165° C/Gas Mark 3.
2. Using cooking spray or lining with parchment paper, prepare a 9 x 13 inch baking pan. Transfer the dough from mixing the bowl to the center of your pan and spread evenly.
3. Place pan in the middle of the oven and bake for 45 minutes.
4. When a knife blade or toothpick comes out clean, remove pan from oven and set on a cooling rack.
5. Once completely cooled, cut into 32 even pieces. This may be done in the pan. Alternatively, the entire non-cut baked good can be removed from the pan and cut on a cutting board. Store in a tightly sealed container.

TIPS & THOUGHTS
If working with fresh berries, you may find that they release juice. Consider collecting this liquid and put it into the dough in place of the lemon juice.

Instead of strawberries think of other berries you might use. Blueberries and lemon are supposed to be a tasty combination – who knows, maybe kiwi! Let me know what you try and most enjoy.

PAIRINGS
Memories ... of summer.

COOKIE SQUARES REFERENCE

| Chocolate Citrus | Chocolate Raspberry | Lemon Citrus | Lemon Lime | Lemon Raspberry |

A NOTE ON DOUBLING MY COOKIE SQUARE RECIPES
As you read at the end of the Biscotti chapter, for the sake of efficient production I doubled certain recipes while producing cookies in the Whidbey Island Baking Company bakery.

I regularly doubled the following Cookie Square recipes with consistently good results – Espresso Chocolate Chip and Lemon.

I have not tried doubling these recipes however I believe they should turn out well – Almond Cranberry, Brunettie, Butterscotch Blondie Coffee, Chocolate Chip, Chocolate Peppermint, Cranberry-Orange, Double Chocolate, and Strawberry Lemonade.

FLAVOUR VARIATIONS
Chocolate Citrus – Make the Double Chocolate Cookie Square recipe, using pure orange extract instead of vanilla extract. Alternatively, you may wish to use white chocolate chips; I believe I have always made this with regular chocolate chips.

Chocolate Raspberry – Make the Double Chocolate Cookie Square recipe using pure raspberry extract instead of vanilla – and, again, I suggest white chips. The raspberries I am accustomed to in the Pacific Northwest tend to be sassy, and the extracts I have used tended to be sweeter and do not produce the chocolate/raspberry flavour I have in mind. Making this combination using raspberry paste might better achieve this effect. Another option to try is to replace 1 cup of the chocolate chips with 1 cup of frozen raspberries and increase your bake time by about 10 minutes.

Lemon Citrus – A tasty mistake I admit to making once … I was in the WIBC bakery making a batch of Lemon Cookie Squares. In my fast pace, I accidentally grabbed and used pure orange extract instead of lemon. As my mixer completed my error I could smell that something was not right – and yet it smelled *GOOD!* So I finished and baked the batch and made another that was correct. I then took my happy accident home – YUM! To help indicate which batch was my 'wrong' batch I sprinkled some dried cranberries on top. If you enjoy the Lemon Cookie Squares, I am pretty sure you're going to love Lemon Citrus Cookie Squares.

Lemon Lime – Make the Lemon Cookie Square recipe as it reads, however, switch the 5 tablespoons lemon juice for lime juice – easy! This gives a subtle flavour and makes a nice cookie. I like to substitute 1 cup of the white chips for sliced almonds that I sprinkle on top.

Lemon Raspberry – Sounds good, right? Yeah, I thought so, too – so I finally got to try it with some homegrown raspberries right before publishing this book – and they were *GREAT!* Similar to my suggestion in the recipe – I swapped 1 cup of white chocolate chips with frozen raspberries and increased the bake time by about 10 minutes. Want more raspberry flavour? Switch the lemon extract for raspberry, of course.

HOW TO SPREAD COOKIE SQUARES

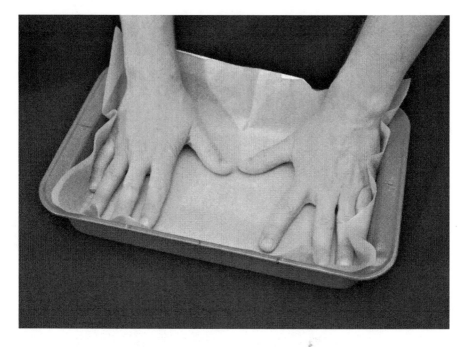

Prepare a 9 x 13 inch baking pan using cooking spray or lining it with parchment paper.

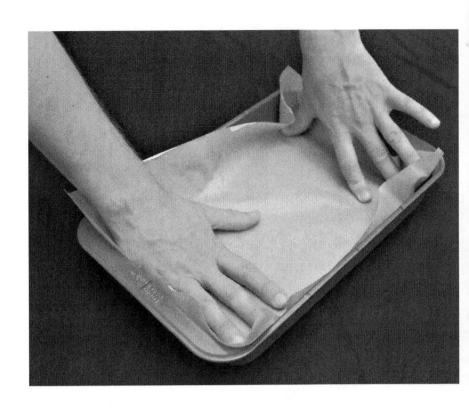

Transfer the dough from mixing the bowl to the center of your pan and spread evenly.

If using parchment paper, it is easier to anchor the paper at one end of the bakeware with your thumb or a finger while pushing the dough in the opposite direction.

Spread dough evenly.

HOW TO CUT COOKIE SQUARES

Once completely cooled, cut the 9 x 13 inch cookie into 32 even pieces. This may be done in the pan. Alternatively, the entire non-cut baked good can be removed from the pan and cut on a cutting board.

Start by making eight guide marks in the 9 x 13 inch cookie using a paring knife – one at the middle of each 9 inch end and three each equally spaced along the 13 inch sides.

Align a large knife with the guide cuts and make four straight cuts across the cookie.

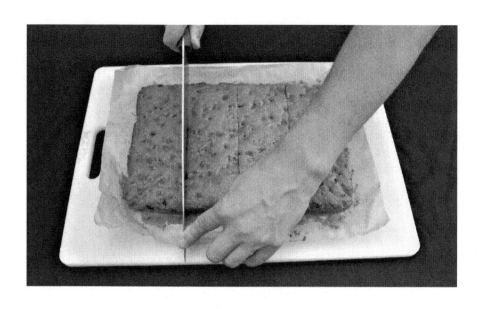

Make two more 13 inch cuts and four 9 inch cuts to produce 32 cookies.

HOW TO CUT
DIAMOND SHAPED COOKIE SQUARES

Cutting cookies like these into diamonds is easy to do and fun to serve.

Once completely cooled, use a paring knife to make the first eight guide marks as indicated in the previous grid-cut instructions "How To Cut Cookie Squares".

Follow by making another twelve cut-marks between these first eight. In total you will have three marks on the 9 inch edges and seven marks along the 13 inch edges.

Using a large knife, make your first series of cuts using the seven pairs of guide marks on the 13 inch sides.

The following cuts are going to be at approximately a 45° angle. With one of the 13 inch sides closest to you pick one of the bottom corners. Align your large knife with the first guide mark on the 13 inch side with the closest guide mark on the 9 inch side and make a cut.

Repeat this with the next two guide marks. The fourth guide mark on the 13 inch side closet to you will align with the far corner of the original 9 x 13 inch cookie.

Continue with aligning the guide marks on the same 45° angle and making cuts.

BISCOTTI

| Anise | Anise-Almond | Cranberry Orange | Double Chocolate | Espresso | Ginger Citrus | Lemon Cake | Peanut Butter | Pumpkin Pie | Toasted Almond | Chocolate Citrus | Chocolate Peppermint | Chocolate Raspberry | Lemon Citrus | Lemon Lime | Almond Chocolate Marble | Mocha Marble | Tiger Eye AKA Peanut Butter Chocolate Marble |

GROWING UP IN ITALY

Biscotti are a true Italian tradition. The word "Biscotti" simply translates into the English word for "cookies" – but they are so much more than that. Biscotti paired with a nice cappuccino in the morning or with an espresso after dinner is perfection! In Italy a traditional breakfast includes variations of biscotti with Cappuccino, tea or warm milk. In the afternoon or with dinner they are paired only with espresso – and they compliment each other wonderfully!

My personal favorite is the classic almond biscotti – not too sweet, just superb balance of flavor. Just simple ingredients like flour, vanilla, eggs, and almonds – a light, subtle flavor that's just perfect. When you dip one into a genuine Italian espresso, it's such a compliment of flavor, it's heavenly. I find this true for all the flavors – lemon, chocolate, anise-almond, *e tanti altri*.

I have so many memories of sitting in Italy surrounded by mountains in a stunning tiny Italian village and being at the local cafe with my biscotti and espresso reading a book. Everything complimented each other. The ambiance ... the people ... the scenery ... it was idyllic, as though I was sitting in a movie.

When I'm in a big city at a cafe with my biscotti and cappuccino, I love to sit back and people watch and take in the culture. Biscotti are baked right into the Italian culture – they are truly part of the essence!

Giovanna ~ Georgia, USA

ANISE BISCOTTI
"Let's try this too and see how it turns out."
– D.P. Scoby, 06 March 2014,
shortly after creating Toasted Almond Biscotti

Anise is a popular biscotto and considered to be one of the most traditional flavours. Growing up, I enjoyed my mother's time-honoured anise cookies with the winter holidays. As I got more and more into biscotti, I was thrilled to find another way to enjoy this spice throughout the year.

U.S. STANDARD – METRIC	INGREDIENT
4 Tablespoons – 60 ml	Unsalted Butter, chilled and cubed
3/4 cup – 180 ml	White Sugar
2	Large Eggs
2 teaspoons – 10 ml	Pure Anise Extract
1 teaspoon – 5 ml	Water
1 Tablespoon – 15 ml	Anise Seed, lightly ground

| 1 1/2 teaspoons – 7.5 ml | Baking Powder |
| 2 cups – 480 ml | All-Purpose flour |

MIXING

1. In a mixing bowl, combine butter and sugar until it becomes the consistency of sand and small pebbles.
2. Beat in eggs, anise extract, and water. Follow with ground anise seed and baking powder.
3. While mixing, add one cup of flour at a time. Avoid over-mixing the flour; if necessary, stop mixing between making measurements.

ROLLING & BAKING

1. Preheat oven to 325° F/165° C/Gas Mark 3. Dust a baking sheet with flour or line with parchment paper.
2. Divide the dough into equal halves and form each section into a ball.
3. Flour your hands. One at a time, roll each dough ball into a cylinder 8 to 10 inches/20 to 25 centimeters long. Re-flour your hands between rolling each ball or as needed.
4. Position the dough cylinders parallel to one another lengthwise on a baking sheet.
5. Using the heel of your hand, gently press each cylinder into a 1 inch/2.5 centimeters thick loaf. These loaves should be spaced at least 2 inches/5 centimeters apart on the baking sheet.
6. Place the baking sheet in the center of the oven and bake for 40-45 minutes or until lightly toasted.
7. Remove the baking sheet from oven, and carefully transfer loaves to a cooling rack. Let sit for 8 to 10 minutes. If you used flour instead of parchment paper, you might wish to remove any remaining residue on the bottom of the loaf with a brush.
8. Place one of the loaves on the center of a cutting board. With a large sharp knife, use a forward and downward motion to cut slices at a 45° angle 1 inch/2.5 centimeters thick.
9. Return the slices to the baking sheet spacing the pieces equally apart down each side with the cut sides upright.
10. Bake for another 8 to 10 minutes.
11. Remove the baking sheet from the oven and transfer pieces back to a cooling rack. Once cool, serve and enjoy!

Makes about 1 dozen pieces plus 4 end pieces. Store biscotti in a tightly sealed container.

TIPS & THOUGHTS
For a stronger anise flavour, consider replacing the measure of water with anise extract.

To get the most flavour from anise seeds, use fresh seeds and give them a slight grind just before adding to the dough. To learn more about how to grind seeds and spices, please see my writing in the reference section at the end of this chapter.

PAIRINGS
Anything you like. I like my Anise Biscotti with coffee and, I have found, so do other people.

Great ... now I don't feel so weird!

ANISE-ALMOND BISCOTTI

"Let's try this one, too, and see how it turns out."
– DPScoby, 04 February 2016

During the summer of 2015, Whidbey Island Baking Company was a regular vendor at two island farmers' markets. One afternoon while talking with one of my customers, I learned that Anise with Almond is an original flavour in the history of biscotti. Just before starting to write this book I experimented with the combination – and Anise-Almond proved to be an incredibly pleasing marriage of flavours!

U.S. STANDARD – METRIC	INGREDIENT
4 Tablespoons – 60 ml	Unsalted Butter, chilled and cubed
3/4 cup – 180 ml	White Sugar
2	Large Eggs
1 teaspoons – 5 ml	Pure Anise Extract
1 teaspoons – 5 ml	Pure Almond Extract
1 teaspoon – 5 ml	Water
1 Tablespoon – 15 ml	Anise Seed, lightly ground
1 1/2 teaspoons – 7.5 ml	Baking Powder
2/3 cup – 160 ml	Almonds, sliced or chopped
2 cups – 480 ml	All-Purpose flour

MIXING

1. In a mixing bowl, combine butter and sugar until it becomes the consistency of sand and small pebbles.
2. Beat in eggs, anise and almond extracts, and water. Follow with ground anise seed, baking powder, and 1/3 cup/80 milliliters almonds.
3. While mixing, add one cup of flour at a time. Avoid over-mixing the flour; if necessary, stop mixing between making measurements.

ROLLING & BAKING
1. Preheat oven to 325° F/165° C/Gas Mark 3. Dust a baking sheet with flour or line with parchment paper.
2. Divide the dough into equal halves and form each section into a ball, then set these aside.
3. Pile 1/6 cup/40 milliliters of the remaining almonds on your cookie sheet. Flour your hands. Roll one of the dough balls on the nuts into a cylinder 8 to 10 inches/20 to 25 centimeters long. Re-flour your hands if necessary and do the same with the other dough ball.
4. Position the dough cylinders parallel to one another lengthwise on a baking sheet.
5. Using the heel of your hand, gently press each cylinder into a 1 inch/2.5 centimeters thick loaf. These loaves should be spaced at least 2 inches/5 centimeters apart on the baking sheet.
6. Place the baking sheet in the center of the oven and bake for 40-45 minutes or until lightly toasted.
7. Remove the baking sheet from oven, and carefully transfer loaves to a cooling rack. Let sit for 8 to 10 minutes. If you used flour instead of parchment paper, you might wish to remove any remaining residue on the bottom of the loaf with a brush.
8. Place one of the loaves on the center of a cutting board. With a large sharp knife, use a forward and downward motion to cut slices at a 45° angle 1 inch/2.5 centimeters thick.
9. Return the slices to the baking sheet spacing the pieces equally apart down each side with the cut sides upright.
10. Bake for another 8 to 10 minutes.
11. Remove the baking sheet from the oven and transfer pieces back to a cooling rack. Once cool, serve and enjoy!

Makes about 1 dozen pieces plus 4 end pieces. Store biscotti in a tightly sealed container.

TIPS & THOUGHTS
To get the most flavour from anise seeds, use fresh seeds and give them a slight grind just before adding to the dough. To learn more about how to grind seeds and spices, please see my writing in the reference section at the end of this chapter.

The almond and anise extracts enhance the flavour of this recipe in addition to the almonds and ground anise seed. If you want a stronger flavour, experiment with substituting the measure of water with either of the extracts or a combination of the two.

PAIRINGS
Anything you like and also with coffee.

CRANBERRY ORANGE BISCOTTI

I thought this up while speaking with Belinda on 04 February 2016 in Bayview – Thanks, Belinda!

One of the great joys I find in baking is in talking with other people about recipe ideas – especially when it is with other bakers. Early in 2016 while making a WIBC baked goods delivery to Whidbey Island's Goose Grocery, I stopped to talk with their grocery manager. Belinda made comments that lead me to experiment with making orange flavoured biscotti with dried cranberries. I brought samples to her the next week, and she asked how soon she could stock my Cranberry Orange Biscotti. Belinda, *this one's for you!*

U.S. STANDARD – METRIC	INGREDIENT
4 Tablespoons – 60 ml	Unsalted Butter, chilled and cubed
3/4 cup – 180 ml	White Sugar
2	Large Eggs
2 Tablespoons – 30 ml	Orange Juice
1-2 teaspoon – 5-10 ml	Pure Orange Extract
2-3 drops	Yellow Food Colouring
2-3 drops	Red Food Colouring
1 1/2 teaspoons – 7.5 ml	Baking Powder
2 cups 2 Tablespoons – 510 ml	All-Purpose Flour
2/3 cup – 160 ml	Dried Cranberries

MIXING
1. In a mixing bowl, combine butter and sugar until it becomes the consistency of sand and small pebbles.
2. Beat in eggs, orange juice, and extract. Follow with food colourings and baking powder.
3. While mixing, add one cup of flour at a time. Avoid over-mixing the flour; if necessary, stop mixing between making measurements.
4. Add the dried cranberries as the last of the flour becomes completely blended.

ROLLING & BAKING

1. Preheat oven to 325° F/165° C/Gas Mark 3. Dust a baking sheet with flour or line with parchment paper.
2. Divide the dough into equal halves and form each section into a ball.
3. Flour your hands. One at a time, roll each dough ball into a cylinder 8 to 10 inches/20 to 25 centimeters long. Re-flour your hands between rolling each ball or as needed.
4. Position the dough cylinders parallel to one another lengthwise on a baking sheet.
5. Using the heel of your hand, gently press each cylinder into a 1 inch/2.5 centimeters thick loaf. These loaves should be spaced at least 2 inches/5 centimeters apart on the baking sheet.
6. Place the baking sheet in the center of the oven and bake for 40-45 minutes or until lightly toasted.
7. Remove the baking sheet from oven, and carefully transfer loaves to a cooling rack. Let sit for 8 to 10 minutes. If you used flour instead of parchment paper, you might wish to remove any remaining residue on the bottom of the loaf with a brush.
8. Place one of the loaves on the center of a cutting board. With a large sharp knife, use a forward and downward motion to cut slices at a 45° angle 1 inch/2.5 centimeters thick.
9. Return the slices to the baking sheet spacing the pieces equally apart down each side with the cut sides upright.
10. Bake for another 8 to 10 minutes.
11. Remove the baking sheet from the oven and transfer pieces back to a cooling rack. Once cool, serve and enjoy!

Makes about 1 dozen pieces plus 4 end pieces. Store biscotti in a tightly sealed container.

TIPS & THOUGHTS

Bottled orange juice should more than adequately serve in this recipe. If you are juicing an orange, consider experimenting with different types of oranges to find a preferred flavour. For an additional boost, zest the orange before juicing and include the zest in the dough.

For a different flavour combination try substituting chopped almonds or roasted pecans in place of the cranberries. Hmm ... coarsely chopped pistachios?

PAIRINGS

I have only made this a few times and consumed it unaccompanied. I imagine this Cranberry-Orange Biscotti would pair well with a cup of Earl Grey or your favourite black tea. Try different things and let me know your suggestions for my next book.

DOUBLE CHOCOLATE BISCOTTI
My first biscotti recipe!

Many people enjoy chocolate, and often the only thing better than chocolate is more chocolate! So when I first tried my hand at biscotti, I found a chocolate recipe and got to work. In the process I made two mistakes – I used cold butter and only half of what the recipe called for – these 'mistakes' became attributes to how I make biscotti. I have crafted many of my other recipes based off of my Double Chocolate Biscotti, and it therefore remains as one of the most important in my collection.

U.S. STANDARD – METRIC	INGREDIENT
4 Tablespoons – 60 ml	Unsalted Butter, chilled and cubed
3/4 cup – 180 ml	White Sugar
2	Large Eggs
2 Tablespoons – 30 ml	Strong Coffee or Espresso
1 teaspoon – 5 ml	Pure Vanilla Extract
1 1/2 teaspoons – 7.5 ml	Baking Powder
1/3 cup – 80 ml	Unsweetened

	Cocoa Powder
2 cups 2 Tablespoons – 510 ml	All-Purpose Flour
2/3 cup – 160 ml	Semi-Sweet Chocolate Chips

MIXING

1. In a mixing bowl, combine butter and sugar until it becomes the consistency of sand and small pebbles.
2. Beat in eggs, coffee, and vanilla extract. Follow with baking powder and unsweetened cocoa powder.
3. While mixing, add one cup of flour at a time. Avoid over-mixing the flour; if necessary, stop mixing between making measurements.
4. Add the chocolate chips as the last of the flour becomes completely blended.

ROLLING & BAKING

1. Preheat oven to 325° F/165° C/Gas Mark 3. Dust a baking sheet with flour or line with parchment paper.
2. Divide the dough into equal halves and form each section into a ball.
3. Flour your hands. One at a time, roll each dough ball into a cylinder 8 to 10 inches/20 to 25 centimeters long. Re-flour your hands between rolling each ball or as needed.
4. Position the dough cylinders parallel to one another lengthwise on a baking sheet.
5. Using the heel of your hand, gently press each cylinder into a 1 inch/2.5 centimeters thick loaf. These loaves should be spaced at least 2 inches/5 centimeters apart on the baking sheet.
6. Place the baking sheet in the center of the oven and bake for 40-45 minutes or until lightly toasted.
7. Remove the baking sheet from oven, and carefully transfer loaves to a cooling rack. Let sit for 8 to 10 minutes. If you used flour instead of parchment paper, you might wish to remove any remaining residue on the bottom of the loaf with a brush.
8. Place one of the loaves on the center of a cutting board. With a large sharp knife, use a forward and downward motion to cut slices at a 45° angle 1 inch/2.5 centimeters thick.

9. Return the slices to the baking sheet spacing the pieces equally apart down each side with the cut sides upright.
10. Bake for another 8 to 10 minutes.
11. Remove the baking sheet from the oven and transfer pieces back to a cooling rack. Once cool, serve and enjoy!

Makes about 1 dozen pieces plus 4 end pieces. Store biscotti in a tightly sealed container.

TIPS & THOUGHTS
My preference is to make this recipe with dark cocoa powder. To reduce cost, yet retain much of the same flavour and colour, I have used a blend of equal parts dark and regular cocoa powders.

To add a visual and subtle flavour dimension to this recipe, when rolling the dough balls into cylinders, roll each ball in about 1/6th cup/80 milliliters sliced almonds.

PAIRINGS
Hey, it's chocolate – how can you go wrong?!?

ESPRESSO BISCOTTI
Coffee coffee coffee!

Right now coffee is **BIG** – perhaps bigger than ever! Bean fans and non-fans have told me they enjoy this recipe. This is the second recipe I made – and of course, everything is better with chocolate, so I added chips to give it a bit of a mocha hint ...

U.S. STANDARD – METRIC	INGREDIENT
4 Tablespoons – 60 ml	Unsalted Butter, chilled and cubed
3/4 cup – 180 ml	White Sugar
2	Large Eggs
2 Tablespoons – 30 ml	Strong Coffee or Espresso
1 teaspoon – 5 ml	Pure Vanilla Extract
1 1/2 teaspoons – 7.5 ml	Baking Powder
3 Tablespoons – 45 ml	Coffee, ground
2 cups 2 Tablespoons – 510 ml	All-Purpose Flour

2/3 cup – 160 ml..Semi-Sweet
                                                    Chocolate Chips

MIXING
1. Make strong coffee or espresso and set aside.
2. In a mixing bowl, combine butter and sugar until it becomes the consistency of sand and small pebbles.
3. Beat in eggs, liquid coffee, and vanilla extract. Follow with baking powder and ground coffee.
4. While mixing, add one cup of flour at a time. Avoid over-mixing the flour; if necessary, stop mixing between making measurements.
5. Add the chocolate chips as the last of the flour becomes completely blended.

ROLLING & BAKING
1. Preheat oven to 325° F/165° C/Gas Mark 3. Dust a baking sheet with flour or line with parchment paper.
2. Divide the dough into equal halves and form each section into a ball.
3. Flour your hands. One at a time, roll each dough ball into a cylinder 8 to 10 inches/20 to 25 centimeters long. Re-flour your hands between rolling each ball or as needed.
4. Position the dough cylinders parallel to one another lengthwise on a baking sheet.
5. Using the heel of your hand, gently press each cylinder into a 1 inch/2.5 centimeters thick loaf. These loaves should be spaced at least 2 inches/5 centimeters apart on the baking sheet.
6. Place the baking sheet in the center of the oven and bake for 40-45 minutes or until lightly toasted.
7. Remove the baking sheet from oven, and carefully transfer loaves to a cooling rack. Let sit for 8 to 10 minutes. If you used flour instead of parchment paper, you might wish to remove any remaining residue on the bottom of the loaf with a brush.
8. Place one of the loaves on the center of a cutting board. With a large sharp knife, use a forward and downward motion to cut slices at a 45° angle 1 inch/2.5 centimeters thick.
9. Return the slices to the baking sheet spacing the pieces equally apart down each side with the cut sides upright.

10. Bake for another 8 to 10 minutes.
11. Remove the baking sheet from the oven and transfer pieces back to a cooling rack. Once cool, serve and enjoy!

Makes about 1 dozen pieces plus 4 end pieces. Store biscotti in a tightly sealed container.

TIPS & THOUGHTS
When I make this recipe at home, I grind the required amount of coffee beans and brew the needed liquid coffee in an espresso maker – and then re-use the grounds in making the dough. I have also used the grounds from my morning coffee, which is convenient as I use a French press. Call me frugal or call me practical, this seems to make the biscotti taste the same as using non-brewed grounds and does not seem to add noticeable moisture to the dough.

Add a hint of nut flavour by substituting vanilla extract with almond extract. Some people like coffee and lemon – instead of vanilla, try using lemon extract!

On occasion, there has been feedback that people dislike the texture of the ground coffee. While a bit of the visual character would be lost from these biscotti, about 1 to 2 Tablespoons of mocha paste can be used instead.

PAIRINGS
More coffee! Okay – joking aside – with the chocolate chips included in this recipe, I have most enjoyed this Espresso Biscotti in the classic combination of milk and cookies. Enjoy!

GINGER CITRUS BISCOTTI

This may be my favourite biscotto recipe – and that of the many people who have tried it. Candied ginger, citrus, molasses, and spices ... oh yes, it is every bit as good as it sounds!

My Ginger Citrus Biscotti recipe carries a simple and yet special story for me ... Around the 2012 winter holidays, I got the idea of gingerbread themed biscotti. During the following January, on a typical cold and wet Pacific Northwest afternoon, my mom and I developed this recipe in the kitchen of the family house. I still imagine a Gingerbread Biscotti – perhaps I will create it and include it in my next book.

U.S. STANDARD – METRIC	INGREDIENT
4 Tablespoons – 60 ml	Unsalted Butter, chilled and cubed
1 cup – 240 ml	Brown Sugar, packed
2	Large Eggs
2 Tablespoons – 30 ml	Dark Molasses
2 teaspoon – 10 ml	Pure Orange Extract
1/2 teaspoon – 2.5 ml	Allspice
1/2 teaspoon – 2.5 ml	Cinnamon
2 teaspoon – 10 ml	Ground Ginger
1 1/2 teaspoons – 7.5 ml	Baking Powder
2 1/4 cups – 540 ml	All-Purpose Flour
2/3 cup – 160 ml	Candied Ginger, chopped

MIXING

1. In a mixing bowl, combine butter and sugar until it becomes the consistency of sand and small pebbles.
2. Beat in eggs, molasses, and extract. Follow with allspice, cinnamon, ground ginger, and baking powder.
3. While mixing, add one cup of flour at a time. Avoid over-mixing the flour; if necessary, stop mixing between making measurements.
4. Add the chopped candied ginger as the last of the flour becomes completely blended.

ROLLING & BAKING

1. Preheat oven to 325° F/165° C/Gas Mark 3. Dust a baking sheet with flour or line with parchment paper.
2. Divide the dough into equal halves and form each section into a ball.
3. Flour your hands. One at a time, roll each dough ball into a cylinder 8 to 10 inches/20 to 25 centimeters long. Re-flour your hands between rolling each ball or as needed.
4. Position the dough cylinders parallel to one another lengthwise on a baking sheet.
5. Using the heel of your hand, gently press each cylinder into a 1 inch/2.5 centimeters thick loaf. These loaves should be spaced at least 2 inches/5 centimeters apart on the baking sheet.
6. Place baking sheet in the center of the oven and bake for 40-45 minutes or until lightly toasted. While waiting play bagpipes.
7. Remove the baking sheet from oven, and carefully transfer loaves to a cooling rack. Let sit for 8 to 10 minutes. If you used flour instead of parchment paper, you might wish to remove any remaining residue on the bottom of the loaf with a brush. Otherwise, practice bagpipes more.
8. Place one of the loaves on the center of a cutting board. With a large sharp knife, use a forward and downward motion to cut slices at a 45° angle 1 inch/2.5 centimeters thick.
9. Return the slices to the baking sheet spacing the pieces equally apart down each side with the cut sides upright.
10. Bake for another 8 to 10 minutes. This is the last chance to get in some bagpipe practice time.
11. Remove baking sheet from oven and transfer pieces back to a cooling rack. While cooling, practice ... ehh, you know the drill.

Makes 12 to 18 pieces plus 4 end pieces. Store Ginger Citrus Biscotti in a tightly-sealed and cleverly-concealed container as anyone who knows about these will likely eat them all.

TIPS & THOUGHTS

NOTE – The ability to play bagpipes of any form or skill level is not a requirement for producing this recipe. In my experience, playing pipes or recordings of bagpipes – or not – does not seem to affect the quality of the finished biscotti. This is a detail I wrote into the recipe when it was created, which I did to amuse myself – oh, and I did play pipes during those baking periods.

Originally I made this recipe with 2 Tablespoons/30 milliliters of fresh orange or lemon zest. I preferred orange only because after zesting it I could eat the orange (of course, not while playing bagpipes). Just before launching WIBC I decided to change the recipe to 2 teaspoons/10 milliliters of pure orange extract to make production more efficient in the bakery. Either extract or zest should work in your home kitchen.

For an enhanced appearance and subtle additional flavour roll your dough in sliced or chopped almonds. Applying the same technique as found with my Toasted Almond Biscotti, use 1/3rd cup/80 milliliters of nuts per batch of Ginger Citrus Biscotti.

As said, this may be my favourite biscotti recipe and it has shown to be popular among many people who have tried it. I have seen people savor a piece and then, when they think I'm not looking, stash away a few more pieces for later. Yes, people have actually *'stolen'* my biscotti. It remains an odd yet remarkable compliment – don't be surprised if it happens to you, too!

PAIRINGS
In addition to tea and coffee, I would suggest trying this with hot apple cider or hot chocolate.

LEMON CAKE BISCOTTI
Do you like lemon? I like lemon!

Lemon goodies always get my attention. As my interest developed in making biscotti, I wanted to create a cookie with a similar taste to lemon meringue pie. When my first attempt produced only a subtle flavour I sought the opinion of my friends Jim & Annette. They were quite pleased – enough to where Annette proclaimed that previously my Ginger Citrus Biscotti was her favourite, but now there was a tie. When I told them that I was disappointed and thought to scratch the recipe they both said *"NO!"* Annette suggested that the flavour was delicate, that the recipe was a keeper, and I should call it Lemon Cake Biscotti – and Jim agreed. Then it all made sense – and the rest is WIBC biscotti history. *Thanks, Annette & Jim!*

U.S. STANDARD – METRIC	INGREDIENT
4 Tablespoons – 60 ml	Unsalted Butter, chilled and cubed
3/4 cup – 180 ml	White Sugar
2	Large Eggs
2 Tablespoons – 30 ml	Lemon Juice
1-2 teaspoons – 5-10 ml	Pure Lemon Extract
3-6 drops	Yellow Food Colouring
1 1/2 teaspoons – 7.5 ml	Baking Powder
2 cups plus 2 Tablespoons – 510 ml	All-Purpose Flour
2/3 cup – 160 ml	White Chocolate Chips

MIXING
1. In a mixing bowl, combine butter and sugar until it becomes the consistency of sand and small pebbles.
2. Beat in eggs, lemon juice, and extract. Follow with yellow food colouring and baking powder.
3. While mixing, add one cup of flour at a time. Avoid over-mixing the flour; if necessary, stop mixing between making measurements.
4. Add the white chocolate chips as the last of the flour becomes completely blended.

ROLLING & BAKING
1. Preheat oven to 325° F/165° C/Gas Mark 3. Dust a baking sheet with flour or line with parchment paper.
2. Divide the dough into equal halves and form each section into a ball.
3. Flour your hands. One at a time, roll each dough ball into a cylinder 8 to 10 inches/20 to 25 centimeters long. Re-flour your hands between rolling each ball or as needed.
4. Position the dough cylinders parallel to one another lengthwise on a baking sheet.
5. Using the heel of your hand, gently press each cylinder into a 1 inch/2.5 centimeters thick loaf. These loaves should be spaced at least 2 inches/5 centimeters apart on the baking sheet.
6. Place the baking sheet in the center of the oven and bake for 40-45 minutes or until lightly toasted.
7. Remove the baking sheet from oven, and carefully transfer loaves to a cooling rack. Let sit for 8 to 10 minutes. If you used flour instead of parchment paper, you might wish to remove any remaining residue on the bottom of the loaf with a brush.
8. Place one of the loaves on the center of a cutting board. With a large sharp knife, use a forward and downward motion to cut slices at a 45° angle 1 inch/2.5 centimeters thick.
9. Return the slices to the baking sheet spacing the pieces equally apart down each side with the cut sides upright.
10. Bake for another 8 to 10 minutes.
11. Remove the baking sheet from the oven and transfer pieces back to a cooling rack. Once cool, serve and enjoy!

Makes about 1 dozen pieces plus 4 end pieces. Store biscotti in a tightly sealed container.

TIPS & THOUGHTS
As I was working to get WIBC off the ground I attended various summer festivals here on Whidbey Island to talk with people about baking and to hand out fliers. While at one of these events I met a fellow who told me about mandelbrot. He explained that he was from New York and could easily find it there but had not seen any in his time on the west coast. It is essentially Jewish biscotti and he suggested that if I included mandlebrot in my lineup I could have something unique in the region. When I researched mandelbrot I found that it is popular among Eastern European Jews and called מאַנדעלברויט in Yiddish, kamishbrot in Ukraine, and mandel bread in English-speaking countries. I also returned to the book that I started making biscotti from to see if it had anything to say about mandelbrot or mandel bread. To my surprise one recipe was presented, so I turned to the page in curious anticipation. Upon reading the ingredients I found that this and my Lemon Cake Biscotti recipe were nearly identical! So, is this Lemon Cake Biscotti or mandelbrot? You decide!

Try something different – swap the white chips in this recipe for chopped candied ginger, coarsely chopped pistachios, or dried berries – anything from cranberries to blueberries, raspberries, blackberries, et cetera. If you know how to cook with lavender, please contact me and share how you would include it in this recipe.

Similar to my Toasted Almond Biscotti recipe, you might enjoy rolling this lemon dough in sliced or chopped almonds. Use about 1/6th cup/40 ml of nuts per loaf.

PAIRINGS
I find that this biscotto is best coupled with a really good cup of coffee. It makes for a classic pairing, like: wine and cheese, Bert & Ernie, peanut butter and jelly, Geb & Nut, chicken and dumplings, Bonnie & Clyde, tea and crumpets, Paul Revere & The Raiders, milk and cookies, Yin & Yang, peas and carrots, Captain & Tennille, apples and oranges, Fred & Barney, ketchup and mustard, Lavern & Shirley, curds and whey, love and marriage, cheese and crackers, Thelma & Louise, meat

and potatoes, or ABBA and KISS in a double-header reunion concert tour.

PEANUT BUTTER BISCOTTI
Defying the notion that all biscotti must be 'fancy'.

There seems to be a stigma that biscotti are strictly elegant. My understanding is that it has rather humble beginnings – serving a similar role as hardtack, it was meant to hold and travel. Whatever the case, sometimes you just want what I call "Good eatin' food" – also known as 'comfort food' – something you can eat and enjoy without formalities, without restrictions. So in the spring of 2013, I created my Peanut Butter Biscotti recipe, and here it is for you to enjoy –
Have At It!

U.S. STANDARD – METRIC	INGREDIENT
4 Tablespoons – 60 ml	Unsalted Butter, chilled and cubed
1 cup – 240 ml	White Sugar
1 cup – 240 ml	Brown Sugar, packed
1 cup – 240 ml	Chunky Peanut Butter
4	Large Eggs
2 teaspoon – 10 ml	Pure Vanilla Extract

1 Tablespoon – 15 ml	Baking Powder
4 cups – 960 ml	All-Purpose Flour

MIXING

1. In a mixing bowl, combine butter and sugars until it becomes the consistency of sand and small pebbles.
2. Beat in peanut butter, eggs, vanilla extract, and baking powder.
3. While mixing, add one cup of flour at a time. Avoid over-mixing the flour; if necessary, stop mixing between making measurements.

ROLLING & BAKING

1. Preheat oven to 325° F/165° C/Gas Mark 3. Dust a baking sheet with flour or line with parchment paper.
2. Divide the dough into equal halves and form each section into a ball.
3. Flour your hands. One at a time, roll each dough ball into a cylinder 8 to 10 inches/20 to 25 centimeters long. Re-flour your hands between rolling each ball or as needed.
4. Position the dough cylinders parallel to one another lengthwise on a baking sheet.
5. Using the heel of your hand, gently press each cylinder into a 1 inch/2.5 centimeters thick loaf. These loaves should be spaced at least 2 inches/5 centimeters apart on the baking sheet.
6. Place the baking sheet in the center of the oven and bake for 40-45 minutes or until lightly toasted.
7. Remove the baking sheet from oven, and carefully transfer loaves to a cooling rack. Let sit for 8 to 10 minutes. If you used flour instead of parchment paper, you might wish to remove any remaining residue on the bottom of the loaf with a brush.
8. Place one of the loaves on the center of a cutting board. With a large sharp knife, use a forward and downward motion to cut slices at a 45° angle 1 inch/2.5 centimeters thick.
9. Return the slices to the baking sheet spacing the pieces equally apart down each side with the cut sides upright.
10. Bake for another 8 to 10 minutes.
11. Remove the baking sheet from the oven and transfer pieces back to a cooling rack. Once cool, serve and enjoy!

Makes about 2 dozen pieces plus 8 end pieces. Store biscotti in a tightly sealed container.

TIPS & THOUGHTS

You will notice that the measurement of each ingredient listed above can be cut in half. These were written this way simply because it is how I have always made the recipe. Here is the good news though when keeping it as written – more cookies! But wait – there's more! Everything is better with chocolate, right? Make this recipe with equal parts Double Chocolate Biscotti dough and marble the two together. I call this Tiger Eye Biscotti due to its finished appearance. Instructions for marbling are found at the end of this chapter.

Instead of marbling, I have added semi-sweet chocolate chips to my Peanut Butter Biscotti. Alternatively, you may wish to add more peanuts.

When some friends of mine were moving out of state, they requested that I make Peanut Butter Bacon Biscotti for their going-away party. I baked and chopped bacon and included it in the dough – I did this with my Double Chocolate Biscotti, too. It proved to be tasty – their guests polished off both batches, with some folks wrapping up a few pieces and leaving with them in their purses and pockets. For either of these modifications, use about 2/3rds cup/160 milliliters of chopped bacon.

Lastly, when I make my Peanut Butter Biscotti I usually do not measure the peanut butter – I just liberally eyeball it.

PAIRINGS
Surprisingly enough – hot apple cider!

PUMPKIN PIE BISCOTTI

This biscotto has proven to be a good fit with entertaining during Thanksgiving and Christmas – but for pumpkin pie and cookie fans, this biscotto is great anytime.

Typically, I encourage baking by the seat of your pants – or the pleats of your kilt as it may be – so it pains me to do this, but let me rein you in for this one. The instructions for preparing a batch of my Pumpkin Pie Biscotti are different than the other recipes found in this chapter, *so read everything carefully before you begin.*

- For some reason, this dough seems to only allow for baking one sheet at a time. While ovens vary, the first baking generally takes 20 minutes and the second baking 15 minutes.
- The dough tends to stick to a floured or parchment paper covered baking sheet. If you are baking multiple batches in succession, you will need to wash your sheet or change paper between each batch.
- It is best if you bake this recipe no more than the day before you plan to serve these biscotti. Even when properly stored, the shelf life of the finished product is much shorter – somewhere around 3 1/2 days. While these cookies will still be perfectly edible, they tend to develop a slight texture issue – simply put they become a little rubbery. I take pride in my baking, and I do not want people to think I made something that is – well … rubbery. In any case, these tend to disappear quickly … people like 'em!

U.S. STANDARD – METRIC	INGREDIENT
4 Tablespoons – 60 ml	Unsalted Butter, chilled and cubed
1 cup – 240 ml	White Sugar
1 cup – 240 ml	Brown Sugar, packed
2	Large Eggs
1/2 cup – 120 ml	Pumpkin Purée
2 teaspoon – 10 ml	Pure Vanilla Extract
2 teaspoons – 10 ml	Baking Powder
1 1/2 teaspoon – 7.5 ml	Cinnamon
1 teaspoon – 5 ml	Nutmeg
1/4 teaspoon – 1.25 ml	Ground Ginger

1/4 teaspoon – 1.25 ml	Ground Cloves
3 3/4 cup – 900 ml	All-Purpose Flour
1/2 to 3/4 cup – 120 to 180 ml	Dried Cranberries
1/2 to 3/4 cup – 120 to 180 ml	Crushed Roasted Pecans

ROASTING PECANS – *DO NOT SKIP THIS*

Roasting AKA toasting brings out the natural complexities and deliciousness of the nuts. Don't believe this? Try eating a pecan followed by eating a *roasted* pecan – the pecan will taste bitter whereas the roasted nut will taste buttery. Besides, the process is simple and quick. Heat your oven to 350° F/175° C/Gas Mark 4 – out of convenience, I usually use my toaster oven. Spread your shelled pecans on a sheet of aluminum foil and place in your oven on a baking sheet for 5-7 minutes or until the pecans become fragrant. Watch the roasting carefully as the pecans can scorch easily.

MIXING

1. In a mixing bowl, combine butter and sugars until it becomes the consistency of sand and small pebbles.
2. Beat in eggs, pumpkin purée, and vanilla extract. Follow with baking powder, cinnamon, nutmeg, ground ginger, and cloves.
3. While mixing, add one cup of flour at a time. Avoid over-mixing the flour; if necessary, stop mixing between making measurements.
4. Add the dried cranberries and pecans as the last of the flour becomes completely blended.

ROLLING & BAKING

1. Preheat oven to 350° F/175° C/Gas Mark 4. Dust a baking sheet with flour or line with parchment paper.
2. Divide dough into thirds or quarters in your mixing bowl with a scraper or knife.
3. Scoop one of the portions of dough onto your sheet, dust your hands with flour. Work Quickly (or as I prefer to say "expeditiously") – this dough is moister than other types of biscotti dough and can soak through the flour on the sheet in the time it takes to flour your hands.

4. One at a time, gently roll each dough ball into a cylinder 8 to 10 inches/20 to 25 centimeters long. Re-flour your hands between rolling each ball or as needed.
5. Position the dough cylinders parallel to one another lengthwise on a baking sheet.
6. Using the heel of your hand, gently press each cylinder into a 1 inch/2.5 centimeters thick loaf. These loaves should be spaced at least 2 inches/5 centimeters apart on the baking sheet.
7. Place a single baking sheet in the center of the oven and bake for 20 to 30 minutes until lightly browned and the center is firm to the touch.
8. Remove baking sheet from oven. Carefully transfer loaves to a cooling rack and let sit for 15 minutes. If you used flour instead of parchment paper, you might wish to remove any remaining residue on the bottom of the loaf with a brush.
9. Reduce oven to 300° F/148° C/Gas Mark 2.
10. Place one of the loaves on the center of a cutting board. With a large sharp knife, use a forward and downward motion to cut slices at a 45° angle 1 inch/2.5 centimeters thick.
11. Return the slices to the baking sheet spacing the pieces equally apart down each side with the cut sides upright.
12. Bake for an additional 15-20 minutes.
13. Remove baking sheet from oven and transfer pieces back to a cooling rack. Once cool, serve and enjoy!

Makes about 1-2 dozen pieces plus 2 end pieces per loaf. Store in a tightly sealed container.

TIPS & THOUGHTS

So now that you have made this Pumpkin Pie Biscotti do you have some leftover canned pumpkin purée? Are you asking yourself what to do with it or if you can freeze it? Well, I can tell you to make a pumpkin pie, pumpkin cheesecake, pumpkin muffins, pumpkin bread, or even pumpkin soup, and that some of these recipes may be in my future books. I can also tell you that *YES* you can freeze leftover pumpkin purée – and here's how and what *not* to do ... which, of course, is what I did the first time I tried it. One option is to simply put the remaining pumpkin purée in a sealable plastic tub and stick it in your freezer. However, this tends to form ice crystals which will later put extra moisture into the purée ... and, yes, this is one of the mistakes

I made. Meā culpā, pumpkin purée – *meā culpā!* The better option is to put the remaining purée into a sealable plastic bag, get as much air out of the bag as you can then seal it, and put this bag-o- purée in your freezer. Now, there is one last thing you should know about using frozen pumpkin purée – and, I admit, is the other detail I skimped on (see "meā culpā" above) – allow the purée to thaw *ENTIRELY* and *MIX IT UP WELL* before using it because the purée will likely have separated. I learned this from a chef. Did I listen? No, not entirely. Did I learn? Yes, the hard way. Lastly, try to use your excess purée within two to three months. In all, this should give you the best results from your leftover purée over just storing it in your fridge.

PAIRINGS
Holidays, friends, picnics, hikes ...

TOASTED ALMOND BISCOTTI

"Let's try this and see how it turns out."
– DPScoby, 04 March 2014

Almond is considered to be another early traditional biscotto flavour. I gave some thought as to how I might make my recipe and decided to base it off of my Double Chocolate Biscotti. One evening, while catching up with a friend on a long phone call, I gave it a go. I nailed the recipe on the first try and it has remained the same ever since!

U.S. STANDARD – METRIC	INGREDIENT
4 Tablespoons – 60 ml	Unsalted Butter, chilled and cubed
3/4 cup – 180 ml	White Sugar
2	Large Eggs
1 teaspoon – 5 ml	Pure Vanilla Extract
1 teaspoon – 5 ml	Pure Almond Extract
1 teaspoon – 5 ml	Water
1 1/2 teaspoons – 7.5 ml	Baking Powder
2 cups – 480 ml	All-Purpose Flour
2/3 cup – 160 ml	Almonds, sliced or chopped

MIXING
1. In a mixing bowl, combine butter and sugar until it becomes the consistency of sand and small pebbles.
2. Beat in eggs, vanilla and almond extracts, and water. Follow with baking powder and 1/3 cup/80 milliliters almonds.
3. While mixing, add one cup of flour at a time. Avoid over-mixing the flour; if necessary, stop mixing between making measurements.

ROLLING & BAKING
1. Preheat oven to 325° F/165° C/Gas Mark 3. Dust a baking sheet with flour or line with parchment paper.
2. Divide the dough into equal halves and form each section into a ball, then set these aside.
3. Pile 1/6 cup/40 milliliters of the remaining almonds on your cookie sheet. Flour your hands. Roll one of the dough balls on the nuts into a cylinder 8 to 10 inches/20 to 25 centimeters long. Re-flour your hands if necessary and do the same with the other dough ball.
4. Position the dough cylinders parallel to one another lengthwise on a baking sheet.
5. Using the heel of your hand, gently press each cylinder into a 1 inch/2.5 centimeters thick loaf. These loaves should be spaced at least 2 inches/5 centimeters apart on the baking sheet.
6. Place the baking sheet in the center of the oven and bake for 40-45 minutes or until lightly toasted.
7. Remove the baking sheet from oven, and carefully transfer loaves to a cooling rack. Let sit for 8 to 10 minutes. If you used flour instead of parchment paper, you might wish to remove any remaining residue on the bottom of the loaf with a brush.
8. Place one of the loaves on the center of a cutting board. With a large sharp knife, use a forward and downward motion to cut slices at a 45° angle 1 inch/2.5 centimeters thick.
9. Return the slices to the baking sheet spacing the pieces equally apart down each side with the cut sides upright.
10. Bake for another 8 to 10 minutes.
11. Remove the baking sheet from the oven and transfer pieces back to a cooling rack. Once cool, serve and enjoy!

Makes about 1 dozen pieces plus 4 end pieces. Store biscotti in a tightly sealed container.

TIPS & THOUGHTS
I specifically prefer to use parchment paper over flouring my baking sheet when it comes to rolling this dough. Flour can cause the almonds to keep from sticking; and after baking the almonds can fall away when dusting the flour off the loaf. If you prefer to roll your dough using flour, it may work better to put the entire measure of almonds in the dough instead.

For a stronger almond flavour, consider replacing the measure of water with additional almond extract.

Try substituting the 1/3 cup/80 milliliters of almonds that go into the dough for dried cranberries. The same amount of dried apple cut into small pieces, other dried fruits, or berries should also produce interesting results. Get creative and experiment! Let me know how it goes.

PAIRINGS
Almond tends to be a neutral flavour that goes well with a variety of hot beverages. I particularly like coupling this with a rich cup of hot chocolate – like something you get around the winter holidays – chocolate/raspberry, chocolate/hazelnut, Dutch chocolate, et cetera.

BISCOTTI REFERENCE

| Chocolate Citrus | Chocolate Peppermint | Chocolate Raspberry | Lemon Citrus | Lemon Lime | Almond Chocolate Marble | Mocha Marble | Tiger Eye Biscotti AKA Peanut Butter Chocolate Marble | Marble Flavours |

A NOTE ON DOUBLING MY BISCOTTI RECIPES

When I was in the Whidbey Island Baking Company bakery, I was in high production. I used commercial size mixers to make 4 to 6 batches of cookies all at the same time. These mixers are similar to what you have at home, just larger and stronger – standing 3 to 5 feet tall on the floor and use a 60-quart bowl.

Sometimes in preparing food, you need to make a bigger supply of a recipe than what one batch will produce. While it is easier and efficient to make two or more batches at once – usually referred to as doubling a batch – for some reason the food does not come out right. Baked goods will fail to rise, food tastes unusual, et cetera.

Of the recipes in this chapter Double Chocolate, Espresso, and Toasted Almond Biscotti have consistently given me good results when doubled. While I have not tried doubling my Anise, Anise-Almond, Cranberry Orange, Ginger Citrus, Lemon Cake, or Peanut Butter Biscotti recipes, I believe these should turn out the same as a single batch. The one recipe I have not doubled and question how it *might* turn out is my Pumpkin Pie Biscotti. My only reason for this is that it features purée which makes it different from all of my other recipes.

ON GRINDING SEEDS AND SPICES

Not familiar with grinding seeds and spices? Let's talk about that...

Grinding helps your seeds and spices to release their natural flavours, and using fresh is always best. There are a number of very simple ways to accomplish this – using a mortar and pestle, a coffee grinder, or a few other effective methods.

Perhaps for most of us, a mortar and pestle are best suited to our needs. They are perfect for crushing small measures of seeds and spices, and produce immediate results while bringing delightful scents to the kitchen. A mortar and pestle is easy to clean – easier than a coffee grinder – usually only requiring a quick wash.

When I was in the Whidbey Island Baking Company bakery, the best choice was a coffee grinder. These can be purchased online and in stores, including secondhand stores. Since most of my time was spent in the bakery, I had two grinders – one for coffee and one for grinding seeds and spices. If you spend a lot of time in the kitchen, a coffee grinder is ideal. It will help if you are grinding a large number of seeds or in making spice blends. Put your measure of seeds or spices into the grinder. Put the lid on and start the grinder – a few seconds should do. Personally, I activate the switch 3-5 times and call it good.

If you only have one grinder and want to keep coffee out of your seeds and spices – and ultimately your biscotti – there is a very simple way to clean it out (alternatively, spice in your coffee can be tasty!). Over-toast a piece of bread – not burnt, just well toasted, crisp and dry. Cut it up into small pieces – about 1x1 centimeter squares – and fill your coffee grinder about half full of these pieces. Run your coffee grinder as you would for coffee and then dump the breadcrumbs out. Repeat until you have used up the whole supply of toasted bread squares. Make sure all of the crumbs are out before grinding any seeds or spices. Your coffee grinder may need to be wiped out with a towel or cloth to get all the crumbs out – *SAFETY FIRST* – unplug your grinder beforehand *EVERY TIME*. A pastry brush with stiff bristles should also suffice depending on what seeds or spices you have ground. If you choose this approach I suggest getting a dedicated brush and marking it "SPICES" – also, keep it dry.

You can apparently also grind seeds using a blender, a pepper mill, or a sealable plastic bag and a hammer. During a few of the famous south Whidbey Island power outages I made due by using two flexible cutting mats and a baseball bat to grind coffee beans. Hey – when you've been without power for four days, you need some comfort food! I have since purchased a hand-powered coffee grinder which is a considerable improvement.

FLAVOUR VARIATIONS
Chocolate Citrus – Make the Double Chocolate Biscotti recipe and instead of using pure vanilla extract use pure orange extract. Alternatively, you may wish to use white chocolate chips; I believe I have always made this with regular chocolate chips.

Chocolate Peppermint – When I first experimented with making Chocolate Peppermint Biscotti I would make a batch of Double Chocolate Biscotti as normal and substitute the chocolate chips with chopped up candy canes around the holidays or peppermint discs which of course are available year-round. Once in production, I did not have time to chop up candy nor could I find a regular supplier of chopped or mini peppermint discs. The easy, effective, and delicious alternative was to use pure peppermint extract in place of the vanilla, and white chocolate chips instead of chocolate chips. Some people would tell me that they thought the white chips took on the peppermint flavour, which then made them similar to including chopped up peppermint candies.

Chocolate Raspberry – Make the Double Chocolate Biscotti recipe substituting the pure vanilla extract with raspberry extract. Again, you may wish to use white chocolate chips in place of chocolate chips.

Lemon Citrus – Make the Lemon Cake Biscotti recipe as normal, substituting orange juice in place of the lemon juice.

Lemon Lime – Make the Lemon Cake Biscotti recipe as normal, substituting lime juice in place of the lemon juice. And now that you know how to make Lemon Citrus or Lemon Lime Biscotti, the trick is deciding what to do with your food colouring options ... orange, green, or just stick with yellow?

Pumpkin Pie Biscotti Alternatives – Did you like my Pumpkin Pie Biscotti? I developed similar Blackberry, Blueberry, and Raspberry Biscotti recipes, and intended to include them in this book. However, I only prepared them a few times each a number of years ago. While my results were *quite successful*, when writing this book I chose only to publish recipes that I know work and turn out deliciously when prepared correctly. As I prefer to work with berries when they are in season, I did not have time to re-familiarize myself with making and baking these recipes. One person who tried my Pumpkin Pie Biscotti suggested that by merely omitting the purée and adding a spice or two I could make Chai Biscotti – I would certainly like to try this! Keep an eye on WhidbeyIslandBaking.com for announcements about my future baking books and other delightful recipes!

MARBLE TECHNIQUE AND FLAVOURS

MARBLE TECHNIQUE

Marbling recipes make for impressive looking biscotti and blends of flavours for you and your friends to enjoy. It can also stump non-bakers as to how several different flavours were made together when the necessary step is quite easy.

Start with making your two selected recipes – or perhaps more depending on your creativity. There is no need to wash your mixing parts between batches since the dough will get marbled together. I recommend separating the dough flavours into equal dough balls as you usually would with making a batch – so in most cases this means you will have four dough balls – this makes the marbling easier to manage. Take one ball of each flavour and press them together until they are about 3 inches/7-8 centimeters thick. Rip this apart at a cross-section then stack the pieces back together alternating the flavours of dough. Continue to pull apart the dough, stack and press it back together until you like how it appears. I suggest this pull-apart/stack/press-together technique and urge you to avoid smearing the dough between your hands – smearing blends the two flavours and blurs the finished appearance. Once you are satisfied with the marbling, separate your marbled dough back into two balls – when complete you should have four marbled dough balls. Roll and press the dough as usual in preparing a single batch of biscotti.

Depending on the marble combination I will make flavours in a particular order and chill the first dough as I am crafting the second. Usually chilling can make my biscotti dough difficult to work with, even causing challenges in forming (rolling and pressing) the loaves. This can be an aid, however, with recipes that tend to be moister such as Espresso and Almond. Usually I will put my dough in another bowl, cover the bowl with cling wrap, and stick it in the freezer. Also, bear in mind that while slowed in a refrigerator or freezer the baking powder in your dough is still reacting, so I suggest baking all of your dough close together and not waiting until the next day or later.

Try marbling different recipes that you think would blend well together – this is only limited to your creativity and is directed by your palate.

MARBLE FLAVOURS

Almond Chocolate Marble – Make one batch Toasted Almond and one batch Double Chocolate Biscotti. As these are equal size batches, you can marble some or all of your dough the same as with Mocha Marble. When I produce these biscotti commercially, I did not roll the marbled dough in sliced almonds; however, you may find that you prefer to.

Mocha Marble – This was the first marble biscotti I made, and as such it uses the first two recipes I made. Make one batch each Double Chocolate and Espresso (with chocolate chips) biscotti. Marble all of your dough to make four tasty loaves-worth. Alternatively, you may wish to marble only half of the chocolate and espresso dough together leaving half of each to come out as normal Double Chocolate and Espresso loaves. This produces variety and the appearance of having made more batches for the same amount of work.

Tiger Eye Biscotti (AKA Peanut Butter Chocolate Marble) – As written, my Peanut Butter Biscotti recipe is a double batch. You may prefer to make a half-batch Peanut Butter and one batch Double Chocolate and marble as usual. I like to call these Tiger Eye biscotti after the chatoyant gemstone by the same name.

Other Marble Possibilities – I thought to try marbling my Lemon Cake and Double Chocolate Biscotti together, as some people enjoy the flavour of lemon and chocolate together (not to mention lemon with coffee) along with marbling my Lemon Cake and Ginger Citrus Biscotti recipes. Do not forget Lemon and Raspberry. I can only encourage you to create and experiment with what you think you will enjoy!

HOW TO ROLL BISCOTTI

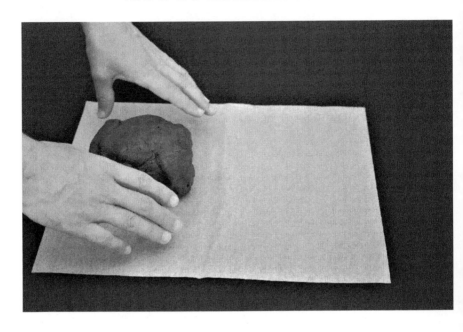

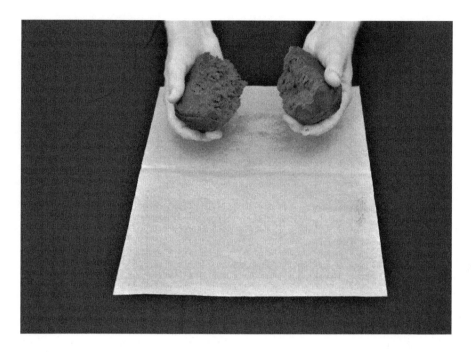

Divide your dough into equal halves and form each section into a ball.

Using both hands, roll each of the dough balls on a baking sheet into cylinders 8 to 10 inches/20 to 25 centimeters long.

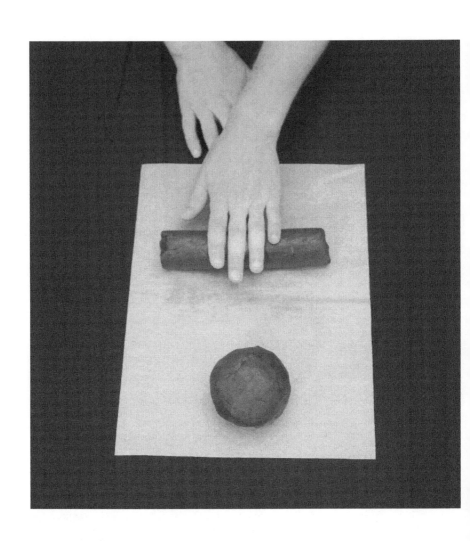

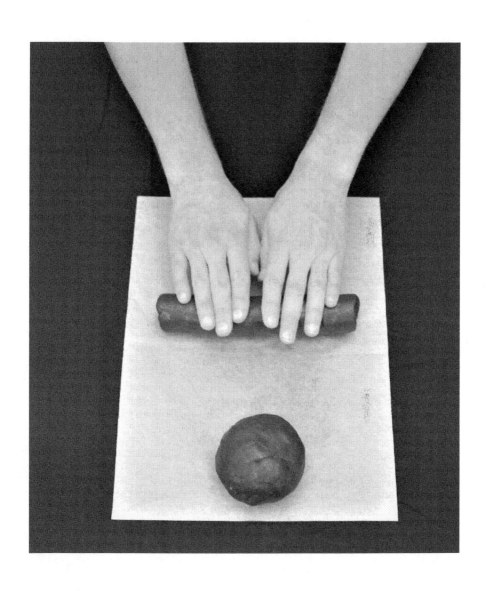

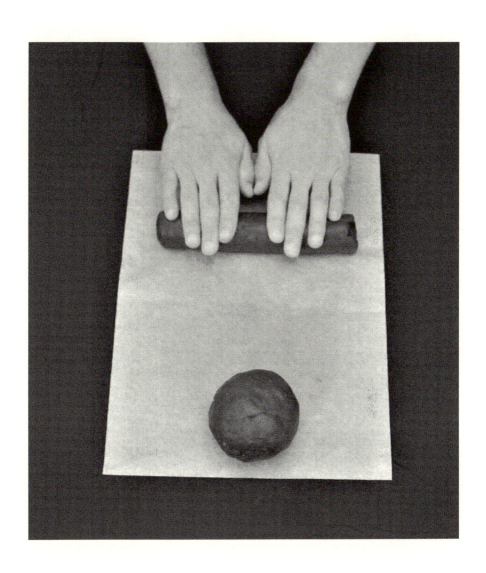

Position the dough cylinders parallel to one another lengthwise on a baking sheet.

Using the heel of your hand, gently press each cylinder into a 1 inch/2.5 centimeters thick loaf.

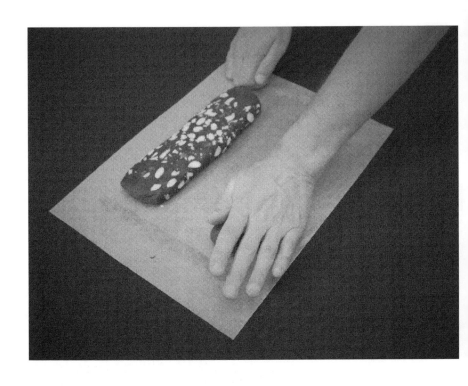

HOW TO ROLL BISCOTTI IN NUTS

Decorating biscotti with nuts starts when rolling the dough.

Divide the dough into equal halves and form each section into a ball, then set these aside.

Pile 1/6 cup/40 milliliters of nuts at the center of your cookie sheet. Roll one of the dough balls on the nuts into a cylinder 8 to 10 inches/20 to 25 centimeters long. Repeat this with the other dough ball.

Position the nut-covered dough cylinders parallel to one another lengthwise on a baking sheet.

Using the heel of your hand, press each cylinder into a 1 inch/2.5 centimeters thick loaf.

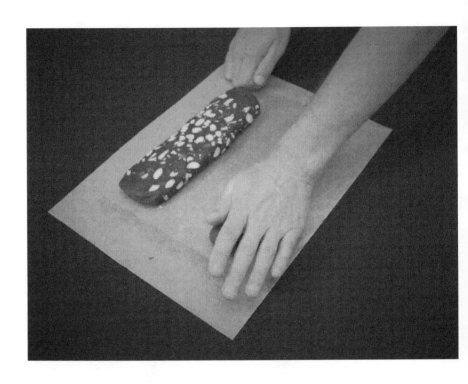

HOW TO CUT BISCOTTI

Place one of the loaves on the center of a cutting board.

With a large sharp knife, use a forward and downward motion to cut slices at a 45° angle 1 inch/2.5 centimeters thick.

Handle the second loaf the same as the first.

Return slices to the baking sheet; space the pieces equally apart with one of their cut sides upright for their second baking.

*You now have The Biscotti Knowledge.
It is a mighty power, and one you must temper with good judgment.*

And remember...

When bribes don't work, use guilt.

MORE COOKIES

| Bigfoot Monster Cookies | Chupacabra Monster Cookies | Cowboy Cookies | Scottish Shortbread | Wrinkles |

GENERATIONS OF BAKING

One of my fondest childhood memories is bursting through the door after school and being met by the fragrance of fresh homemade treats. Warm chocolate chip cookies and cold milk were a sweet indulgence that couldn't be beat!

Christmas cookies are fun to make and eat. I loved the tradition of decorating holiday cookies with my mom, which became a custom enjoyed with my kids. Spending time together being creative makes for special memories. So what if the kitchen gets messy?

Some cookies are comfort foods like the rich buttery taste of shortbread – or our family favorite, anise bars! Brownies and Snicker Doodles are close seconds. I always baked cookies to take along on picnics and camping trips – you never go hungry if there are cookies to munch! Do you have a favorite cookie you turn to as comfort food? Why not make a batch today for someone you love!

                    Lynn ~ Washington, USA

THE ORIGINAL BIGFOOT MONSTER COOKIE
GGRRRRAAARW!!!

Watch kids' faces when you hand them one of these giant cookies!

U.S. STANDARD – METRIC	INGREDIENT
8 Tablespoons – 120 ml	Butter, softened
1 cup – 240 ml	White Sugar
1 cup – 240 ml	Brown Sugar, packed
2 cups – 480 ml	Chunky Peanut Butter
3	Large Eggs
1 teaspoon – 5 ml	Pure Vanilla Extract
2 teaspoons – 10 ml	Baking Soda
4 1/2 cups – 1080 ml	Rolled Oats
1 cup – 240 ml	Semi-Sweet Chocolate Chips
1 cup – 240 ml	Candy Coated Chocolates

MIXING
1. In a mixing bowl, cream butter and sugars.
2. Blend in peanut butter followed by eggs, vanilla extract, and baking soda (bicarbonate of soda).
3. Stir in the chocolate chips and popular colorful candy-coated chocolates followed by the oats.

BAKING
1. Heat oven to 350° F/175° C/Gas Mark 4.
2. Form dough into 1/2 cup/120 milliliters balls and position on a baking sheet with ample space to expand.
3. Flatten to 5 inches/12.5 centimeters wide and dust with sugar.
4. Place baking sheet in the center of the oven and bake for 12 to 18 minutes.
5. Remove baking sheet from oven and carefully transfer the cookies to a cooling rack.

Makes about 14 cookies. Store in a tightly sealed container.

TIPS & THOUGHTS
"Popular Colorful Candy Coated Chocolates" – When I started to explore making monster cookies as part of the Whidbey Island Baking Company line-up, I contacted a certain well-known candy company in regards to using their product in my cookies. From this communication, I developed the impression that if I used their product and/or business name my little baking business could gain the attention of their considerably larger legal department. It remains my opinion that this was *silly*; when they want to stop being silly, then I might consider using their name. In the meantime, you could think to use some round candy-coated chocolates about 1 centimeter in diameter with a name that rhymes with n & n's. Gheesh, Ares, why was that so hard ...?

When I first produced Monster Cookies in the Whidbey Island Baking Company bakery, I made single batches using a 5-quart mixer. I found this bowl size to be a bit on the small side which presented a challenge – during the later stages of mixing the dough usually overflowed while operating the machine. To remedy this, when I reached the end of the ingredients I would mix the oats with the machine, then switch it off and remove the bowl, and finish by mixing the final Bigfoot ingredients by hand.

These cookies freeze well – in my experience, for about two weeks. When I have frozen them, they come directly out of the freezer still chewy – which made a pleasing touch during the summer. Alternatively, you might try using these to make ice cream sandwiches.

You might be able to "cream" the peanut butter in with butter, and then add the eggs, finishing the preparation as directed above.

PAIRINGS
Kids!
(... and kids at heart.)

THE ORIGINAL CHUPACABRA MONSTER COOKIE

BEWARE the Chupacabra – with its red cranberry eyes and its white chocolate chip fangs...

Adults could convince themselves that these Chupacabra Monster Cookies are actually healthy – peanut butter, oats, dried cranberries, and white chocolate chips ... that's practically an energy bar, right?

U.S. STANDARD – METRIC	INGREDIENT
8 Tablespoons – 120 ml	Butter, softened
1 cup – 240 ml	White Sugar
1 cup – 240 ml	Brown Sugar, packed
2 cups – 480 ml	Chunky Peanut Butter
3	Large Eggs
1 teaspoon – 5 ml	Pure Vanilla Extract
2 teaspoons – 10 ml	Baking Soda
4 1/2 cups – 1080 ml	Rolled Oats
1 cup – 240 ml	White Chocolate Chips
1 cup – 240 ml	Dried Cranberries

MIXING
1. In a mixing bowl, cream butter and sugars.
2. Blend in peanut butter followed by eggs, vanilla extract, and baking soda (bicarbonate of soda).
3. Stir in the white chocolate chips and dried cranberries followed by the oats.

BAKING
1. Heat oven to 350° F/175° C/Gas Mark 4.
2. Form dough into 1/2 cup/120 milliliters balls and position on a baking sheet with ample space to expand.
3. Flatten to 5 inches/12.5 centimeters wide and dust with sugar.
4. Place baking sheet in the center of the oven and bake for 12 to 18 minutes.
5. Remove baking sheet from oven and carefully transfer the cookies to a cooling rack.

Makes about 14 cookies. Store in a tightly sealed container.

TIPS & THOUGHTS
As demand for my Whidbey Island Baking Company Monster Cookies grew I usually made four batches of cookies at a time in a large commercial mixer – this worked because the jars of peanut butter I had were 4 pounds / 1.81 kg and I could use the whole jar without measuring. However, when I received orders for single batches of Monster Cookies in the bakery I would use a 5-quart machine – similar to what most people have at home. Working with the smaller machine presented a challenge toward the end of the recipe – the bowl proved to be a bit on the small side with the dough overflowing while the mixer was in operation. Depending on the size of the bowl with your machine, you may want to remove the bowl from the mixer and stir the Chupacabra's white chocolate chips and dried cranberries in by hand.

These cookies freeze well for about two weeks. When I have frozen them, they come directly out of the freezer still chewy – which made a pleasant sensation during summer. Alternatively, you might try using these to make ice cream sandwiches.

To make an ice cream sandwich, you will need two cookies, some ice cream (I prefer vanilla for this), and some plastic wrap. First, let your ice cream warm up to where it is soft and pliable but not to where it has melted. Using a knife or spoon spread a layer of ice cream on the bottom of one of your Monster Cookies about one finger thick. Top this with your other cookie, bottom down, on the ice cream. Completely wrap and seal your sandwich in plastic wrap and stick it back in your freezer for a few hours. When you are ready, take your Monster Ice Cream Sandwich Cookie out of your freezer, unwrap and enjoy!

You might be able to "cream" the peanut butter in with butter, and then add the eggs, finishing the preparation as directed above.

PAIRINGS

Between these two versions of Monster Cookies, I tend to think of the Bigfoot for kids and the Chupacabra for adults. The Bigfoot can pack a bit of a sugar punch while the Chupacabra speaks to more mature tastes. There are of course no 'rules' here. However, you may find that these options can make a better fit for your friends and family. So if you are an "adult" and want to sneak a Bigfoot – *go for it*! And if you want to turn some Chupacabras into an ice cream sandwich ... I won't tell.

COWBOY COOKIES

"What kind of cookies did cowboys eat, Mom?"
... Well, Cowboy Cookies, of course!

Chocolate chip and oatmeal cookies always go over well. They are also an easy cookie for beginning bakers young and old ... I mean, older.

U.S. STANDARD – METRIC	INGREDIENT
16 Tablespoons – 240 ml	Butter, softened (not melted)
3/4 cup – 180 ml	White Sugar
3/4 cup – 180 ml	Brown Sugar, packed
2	Large Eggs
1 teaspoon – 5 ml	Pure Vanilla Extract
1 teaspoon – 5 ml	Baking Soda
1/2 teaspoon – 2.5 ml	Baking Powder
2 1/4 cups – 540 ml	All-Purpose Flour
2 1/4 cups – 540 ml	Oats
12 ounces (about 2 cups) – 340 g	Semi-Sweet Chocolate Chips

MIXING

1. In a mixing bowl, cream the butter followed by mixing in both white and brown sugars.
2. Blend in eggs, vanilla extract, baking soda/bicarbonate of soda, and baking powder.
3. Stir in flour, oats, and chocolate chips.

BAKING

1. Heat oven to 350° F/175° C/Gas Mark 4.
2. Drop spoonfuls of dough onto a baking sheet with space for the dough to expand while baking.
3. Place baking sheet in the center of the oven and bake for 10 to 12 minutes.
4. Remove baking sheet from oven and carefully transfer cookies to a cooling rack.

Makes about 28 cookies. Store in a tightly sealed container if they make it there before people eat these.

TIPS & THOUGHTS
This recipe holds a special place in my baker's heart. One day when I was a kid, I asked my mom an important history question – I wanted to know what kind of cookies cowboys ate. She responded that she didn't know but that she would look in her recipe file to see if something was there. A while later she reported back that she found a recipe titled "Cowboy Cookies" and by the title that must have been the type of cookies cowboys ate. It had oats and chocolate chips, and we could make the recipe if I wanted. I could not have been more pleased! What I did not know was that my mom had, of course, very sweetly selected one of her recipes and rewrote it on an index card with the title "Cowboy Cookies." My family has called the cookie by this name ever since. Suffice to say, my thanks goes to my mom for this fond childhood memory and helping to foster my enjoyment of baking and cooking.

This recipe makes no excuses for being simple to prepare. It is fun and easy to make with kids and good for other beginning bakers. Speaking from experience, if you have a work party at your house, these tend to be received well when folks take breaks.

While this recipe calls for 16 tablespoons of butter, I usually make it with 12-14 tablespoons and can hardly tell the difference.

A friend gave me the suggestion of trying a little spice in the dough – some cinnamon, finely ground coffee, a touch of chili powder or cayenne pepper – just enough to put spurs on the cowboy's boots. Rustle up some of these cookies and let me know how much spice works for you!

You might have noticed that this recipe is based on a 12-ounce bag of chocolate chips. Promise not to tell anyone, but I like putting in about a quarter-bag more.

PAIRINGS
MILK! Friends, picnics, barbeques, hearty hikes, work parties, a rainy day with a book – these cookies are good anytime.

SCOTTISH SHORTBREAD
Simple, buttery, and crispy – shortbread is perfect for any occasion!

U.S. STANDARD – METRIC	INGREDIENT
1 pound – 454 g	Unsalted Butter, room temperature
1 teaspoon – 5 ml	Pure Vanilla Extract (optional)
1 cup – 240 ml	White Sugar
4 cups – 960 ml	All-Purpose Flour

MIXING
1. Just as shortbread has a simple set of ingredients, it is equally simple to make – first by mixer and then finish by hand until the dough is the consistency of "play dough." The following 'instructions' are more a matter of 'tips' as you make the dough.
2. Mix the butter at a moderate speed, getting some air into it, and add the vanilla extract.
3. Then, on low speed, add the sugar to the mixing bowl.

4. Slowly add one cup of flour at a time while continuing on the low speed. Mixers will generally become labored around the point that half of the flour is added. To avoid damage to your machine, mix the rest of the flour by hand – literally – take the bowl off the mixer, roll up your sleeves, pour the remaining flour into the bowl, and go hands-on! This will transition you to the ...

BAKING

1. Take a pinch of dough approximately the size of a ping-pong ball. Roll this into a ball between your palms, applying a little pressure to help the dough meld. Place the ball on a baking sheet and repeat, spacing the balls about 2 inches/5 centimeters apart. There is no need to press the dough balls – during baking they will flatten out on their own, coming out of the oven as half spheres.
2. Bake at 325° F/165° C/Gas Mark 3 for 30 minutes.
3. Lower the oven temperature to 300° F/150° C/Gas Mark 2 and bake for about another 30 minutes. Watch your shortbread closely during the end of this time – this is when the shortbread browns. The browning period is typically short, and the cookies can quickly become overbaked.
4. Once browned, remove the baking sheets from the oven and transfer the cookies to a cooling rack. Allow the shortbread to cool completely before serving.

Makes approximately 36 cookies. Store in a tightly sealed container.

TIPS & THOUGHTS

When it comes to making shortbread, ***do not do what I did*** during my starving-artist days and use margarine. If your margarine package reads 'good for baking,' use it in something else. When I was a fully self-supporting working-musician, I made cookies as a way to afford and participate in gift-giving during the holidays. After making a few rounds of highly disappointing 'shortbread,' I inquired about the difference with a Scottish lady from the local Celtic community – her shortbread was *FANTASTIC!* She kindly sent me a letter with her measurements, instructions, and insight – which included, and to this day I take it as 'lovingly,' correcting me with ***"NO***

SUBSTITUTIONS FOR BUTTER!" With this book, I publicly repent for my use of margarine in Scottish shortbread and will forever atone with unsalted butter. I have been shown the shortbread way, and Margaret Russell, I Thank You.

There is a point in the baking where the shortbread – as I put it – 'turns on.' A truly *WONDERFUL* smell emits from the oven when the butter (thank you again, Margaret) begins to heat. Although shortbread is appropriate year-round, some individuals tend to reserve making it only during the holidays. If this is your preference, do not be surprised if this buttery scent becomes a unique memory associated with winter baking.

Scotland, New Year's Eve, and Shortbread

New Year's Eve in Scotland is referred to as Hogmanay (hog-man-eh). Of the various traditions practiced on this holiday, your home must be clean and organized along with having yourself presentably dressed before midnight, all to make a fresh start on the New Year. Church bells are rung *and then the celebration begins!* People go out into their communities First Footing – visiting their friends' and neighbors' houses. It is good luck for the house if the first person to cross the threshold is a dark-haired male stranger. Traditionally the host offers this guest shortbread for good luck. Visitors are supposed to bring some food or whiskey, some coal or wood, or an instrument to play – these being symbolic of bringing prosperity and good cheer for the year. So make sure you are ready with a batch of Scottish shortbread in your home when the bells ring at midnight!

Want to know more about Hogmanay? Go online or visit your local library!

PAIRINGS & BAGPIPE SHEET MUSIC

Tea, hot chocolate, milk – really anything you like. I enjoy dunking shortbread in my coffee – which somehow feels wrong – however, I like it, and I have heard from other people they do the same.

What could be better than pairing your fresh baked shortbread with some Scottish bagpipes? Please enjoy my personal compositions "Beag air Bheag (Little by Little)", "Lullaby for Zoe" and "Brother Emmett's Waltz" found at the end of this book!

WRINKLES
Easy, tasty, oatmeal and molasses cookies that ...

Disappear

U.S. STANDARD – METRIC	INGREDIENT
1 pound – 454 grams	Unsalted Butter, room temperature
2 cups – 480 ml	Brown Sugar, packed
2 cups – 480 ml	White Sugar
4	Large Eggs
4 teaspoons – 20 ml	Pure Vanilla Extract
4 Tablespoons – 60 ml	Molasses
2 teaspoons – 10 ml	Baking Soda
2 teaspoons – 10 ml	Baking Powder
4 cups – 960 ml	All-Purpose Flour
4 cups – 960 ml	Oats

MIXING
1. Cream butter, brown and white sugars, eggs, vanilla, and molasses.
2. Add baking soda/bicarbonate of soda, baking powder, flour, and oats.

BAKING
1. Drop by teaspoons onto a greased baking sheet about 2 inches/5 centimeters apart.
2. Bake at 350° F/175° C/Gas Mark 4 for 8-10 minutes.
3. While the cookies are still warm, carefully remove them from the baking sheet using a spatula. This will cause them to mash up a bit and give them 'wrinkles'.

This recipe makes a lot of cookies. How many? *A lot*. And then they disappear because they are tasty and chewy, so you almost don't need to concern yourself with how to store them – but if you do need to – as usual, store them in a tightly sealed container.

TIPS & THOUGHTS
This is a family recipe. When I was a kid I gave them the name "Wrinkles" and it stuck. How did I come up with the name "Wrinkles"? If you remove these from your baking sheet using a spatula while they are still warm, they tend to squish a bit and take on 'wrinkles'.

Get ready, here come my LOADS of tips about this recipe ... Use a large mixing bowl, chill the dough before spooning it, and obviously it would be easy to make a half batch.

PAIRINGS
In my experience these cookies disappear – so the 'pairing' would be one cookie in each hand.

MORE COOKIES REFERENCE

A NOTE ON DOUBLING RECIPES FROM THIS CHAPTER

Of the five cookie recipes in this chapter, I developed and marketed two through local stores, farmers markets, festivals and conventions. Here is my experience with doubling these recipes and I believe you should have similar results...

The Original Bigfoot Monster Cookie – This is the first Monster Cookie I made as part of the Whidbey Island Baking Company product line. When I was in the bakery, I was in high production using 30 and 60-quart commercial mixers. I made four batches at a time simply because that matched the contents of one jar of peanut butter. These cookies were a *HIT,* and it was great to receive such a positive response from my customers.

The Original Chupacabra Monster Cookie – As soon as I introduced my Chupacabra Monster Cookies they received the same response my Bigfoot Monster Cookie did. Since they have the exact same base recipe as the Bigfoot they double equally as well.

Scottish Shortbread – Owning a small business and working in a bakery keeps a person *very* busy. Many people consider Scottish Shortbread to be a winter holiday treat, when in actuality it is appropriate and customary to enjoy year round. When I considered marketing my shortbread, I produced four batches so I could make numerous sample bags holding a few pieces each – I wanted to hear from as many people possible as to what they thought. You cannot imagine how it feels when you put four pounds of butter into a commercial mixer ... and how dull it can get making all the individual pieces to go into the oven. Long story short ... Scottish Shortbread, of course, doubles just fine.

Cowboy Cookies – I once doubled the recipe for these hearty cookies for a work party. I heard a lot of happy remarks and no complaints.

Wrinkles – These are a family recipe that I wanted to share through this book. To my recollection, I have never doubled these because they produce so many cookies when only making a single batch. Being a simple recipe, I predict they should double perfectly well.

COFFEE, COFFEE CAKE, AND APPLESAUCE

| French Press Coffee | Flavoured Coffee | Simple Pumpkin Spice Latte | Russian Tea & Friendship Tea | Blueberry Buckle | Slow Cooker Applesauce |

COLLEEN'S COFFEE

From bean to brew, I am a big fan – *a huge fan* – of coffee!

My family tells tales of me at a year and a half old jumping up and down in my crib screaming "Kahki! Kahki!" until I was indulged with what was more cream and sugar than coffee. It appeased me nonetheless.

As I grew older, a cup of coffee grew to represent the company it offered. I remember waking up early in adolescence to the smell of my dad stoking the fire in the wood burner while the percolator bubbled in the kitchen. I have fond memories of gathering in the kitchen for coffee, then breakfast. Memories like this are harder to come by in our hustle-bustle pace where many people set the timer on their coffee maker for when they wake up, program their machine by remote using their smartphone, or seek instant caffeinated gratification from a pod.

As a testament to my love of coffee, we have four coffee makers in my house: a pod machine, a drip coffee maker, a percolator, and a French press. Each has its charms and quirks – and I use them all!

The pod-based machine is instant gratification. The pods vary from coffee, teas, and cocoas to instant powders – flavored, sugared, and pre-powdered creaminess – and it is nice to have a wide selection available. When company comes over, I mix and match depending on my or a guest's mood. Sometimes I make a coffee and a cocoa and mix them into warm mugs. Manufacturers are also introducing iced versions and some soups for these machines. A pod machine would be a nice gift for anyone moving into an apartment or going off to a college dorm room that has minimal space.

Drip coffee makers are good when family comes over, when you need coffee *ASAP* and will be consuming it for a while – like when they come over to play cards and chat. I prefer something a little more full-bodied and strongly flavored with a good hearty medium grind when I'm using the drip coffee maker. The grounds and the hot water are not always together for long enough to get all the flavor and notes from the coffee grounds. (Expert's secret: My mother would always put a few shakes of salt to combat any bitter flavors, and perk up the taste.)

My favorite – and the wonder of my childhood – remains the glass percolator. It is just as beautiful and hypnotizing in its aroma as it is to behold. There is something soothing about watching the bubbles slowly collect, push up through the glass tube, and fountain out at the top to bathe the grounds before returning to the reservoir – and luckily the old wives' rule on watching boiling water does not apply to the glass percolator! The perk should be done on high for the first seven minutes of boil, then lowered to just under medium for another three. Allowing the coffee to rest for two more minutes lets all the water escape from the grounds and filter. Is it a bunch of work? Yep, and it is absolutely worth it! From my home percolator, I get a lovely golden brown cup of clear, smooth coffee, quite worthy of a beautiful glass mug.

I just recently purchased a French press. I wonder why I held off for so long... This method of brewing produces a thick, rich beverage – almost a coffee/cocoa hybrid. I did have to watch a couple videos online and study the instructions a few times, and then I got the hang of it really quickly. Of course, I didn't have Don's instructions found in this chapter.

After brewing, we now have all kinds of creams and milk products, non-dairy options, flavors, syrups, and powders to personalize our cup of coffee. I also enjoy adding spices to my grounds as I am preparing to brew. Ceylon Cinnamon is one of my favorites, as is some freshly shaved nutmeg. Ginger and cardamom are also tasty. Try some cocoa powder added to your grounds – isn't everything better with chocolate?). Then there's good old chicory, which helps with the bitter taste in coffee. Don't let me stop you from getting creative and using up your leftover candy canes to stir it with, or dropping in a piece of chocolate candy or two….

Coffee is a very personal thing; how you like it and how much time you have to spend on it is your choice. The best advice I have for a great cup of coffee is that every once in a while – ENJOY IT! Savor all the subtle nuances that come along with it. Sit down for a sunrise, hold your mug in both hands and inhale... deeply. Look up and savor the company around you, slow down just a tad, listen, enjoy, and make lasting memories.

     Colleen ~ Michigan, USA

HOW TO MAKE GREAT COFFEE USING A FRENCH PRESS
I love my French press!

For those of us who enjoy coffee, usually when we want it – we want it *Now!* Many of us are happy to enjoy a decent daily cup, and yet it is a memorable day when we find that exceptionally good cup of coffee. I am here to say that you can not only have good but *great coffee* every day using a French press ... and a little time.

THE BEST INGREDIENTS PRODUCE THE BEST RESULTS – WATER AND BEANS!

Water and Heat – Tap water will work however it tends to lack the minerals that aid in the extraction process; cold filtered or spring water is considered best. The desired temperature is between 195° F/90.5° C to 205° F/96.1° C (in either case, Gas Mark 1/4).

Beans and Grind – While there are numerous options, I find the best brews come from fresh roasted, shade-grown, certified organic coffee beans. Many people prefer to buy their coffee already ground or to grind it at their store. However, the ideal time to grind is just before brewing. Whatever your preference, get a coarse grind on your beans – this helps to prevent the grounds from reaching your cup after brewing.

THE PROCESS FOR MAKING GREAT FRENCH PRESS COFFEE

Grounds – First you will need to figure out the volume of water your French press holds. You will want a ratio of 2 tablespoons/30 milliliters of ground coffee for every 6 fluid ounces/180 milliliters of water. Through experimentation, you will find if you prefer to use more or fewer coffee grounds for stronger or weaker coffee. When you have the right amount of grounds, take the top or "plunger" portion off your French press and set it aside, and pour your grounds into the bottom of the French press.

Hot Water – Boil sufficient water for your French press then wait for it to cool a little. Once the water has settled should do.

Let's ROCK! ... *I mean,* **Time To Pour** – Pour enough water into the carafe to get onto the grounds. *DO NOT fill the carafe to the top at this time.* The aim is to make a slurry, at most soaking the grounds. Pouring only a little water in and getting the grounds wet – simple, right? Well, this is an essential step in the process of making great French press coffee. There is a trick to pouring the water ... done correctly, you get a visible froth that is about half as dark as the wet grounds beneath it. Most of the time I do not get this froth, so I cheat and swirl my French press around by its handle a few inches off the counter. My understanding is that this froth occurs when some air has gotten into the grounds with pouring the water in, so I figure my swirl-around does the same thing. The next is to ...

Good Things Come To Those Who ... Wait (3 to 5 minutes) – Wait. Yes, *WAIT*. Put the plunger on top of the carafe, depress it an inch or two to help it hold in place, and set your timer for about 3 to 5 minutes. This period is necessary and allows the grounds to bloom. I know, waiting can be a foreign concept (some pun intended).

If you are one of my fellow Americans, for the most of us our lifestyle is go-Go-GO – and when we want coffee, we want it Now! When it comes to making coffee in a French press most of us will dump in our grounds, fill the carafe to the top with water, let it brew for 5 minutes, press, pour, and claim we are cultured because we have used a French press. While that will still make coffee, the method here has for me consistently produced even better-tasting coffee (at least to the attentive palate). With waiting, I am not suggesting that you sit and watch your French press as you produce coffee. No, use the bloom and brew times for something productive – me, I start making breakfast.

That said, moving right along ...

More Water and More Waiting ... Yes, More Waiting – You may wish to bring your water back up to a boil, however as long as you have held it in a kettle or kept it covered the temperature ought to be fine. Remove the plunger assembly and fill the carafe to nearly the top – enough space to put the plunger assembly back on where it can sit on top. As the water gets poured in usually the bloomed grounds will float on top – this may or may not make a difference. Personally, I use the pouring water to sink the grounds. Replace the plunger assembly; again do not depress the plunger, and again WAIT. Yes, for another 3 to 5 minutes and get back to work on making breakfast, meditating on why your life is so stressful, or whatever it is that you do.

Finally – Press, Pour, and Enjoy! Your French press coffee will be at its best during the first 15 minutes.

Conclusion – Slow down and treat yourself a little. Stop and smell the roses ... or in this case, smell the coffee blooming.

And now you can triumphantly proclaim...

"I have a French press* – and I know how to use it!"

* Assuming that you own &/or have a French press in your possession. And if you don't, you can still say that you know how to use it!

FLAVOURED COFFEE
Mmm – TASTY!

Do you enjoy flavoured coffee? Make some yourself! At home or on the go it is easy to add character to your cup with on-hand ingredients.

Use pure extracts, nuts that have been roasted and ground, orange or lemon peel, and spices like cinnamon, nutmeg, or allspice. Simply add 1/4 teaspoon/1.25 milliliters to the coffee grounds when preparing to brew 6 cups/approximately 240 milliliters of your preferred roast.

Experiment with blends to find the right ratio of flavours that suit your taste. Explore and create new combinations to savor and put a personal touch on the coffee you serve. Do-it-yourself flavouring is economical and more convenient than visiting a coffee bar – and should be healthier than many of the sugar syrups commonly used. Give packages of your mixes as gifts or add a unique element to a gift basket of your fresh baked cookies.

TIPS & THOUGHTS
In working on this book, I asked a few friends to 'test drive' this section – I wanted to see that my instructions read well. The feedback I received from Eryn and Colleen was invaluable! Colleen sent her writing that opens this chapter. Eryn surprised me with a note on how she enhances coffee and gave me her permission to write the following ...

Eryn flavours her coffee using essential oils which she adds after brewing. How much oil to add per cup depends on the character of the essential oil. Personally, I am not familiar with this method although it seems perfectly sound – so if you wish to try it, be sure that the oils you use are food grade and safe for consumption. She also surprised me with how to make the Simple Pumpkin Spice Latte found next in this chapter. *Thanks, Eryn!*

PAIRINGS
All the baked goods to make in this book ... but then, dear reader, I am admittedly biased. Experiment with the suggestions above and recipes

in this book – drop me an e-mail as you find matches that prove to be pleasing.

SIMPLE PUMPKIN SPICE LATTE

When Eryn told me about how she flavours coffee with essential oils, she went on to surprise me with another suggestion – how to make a homemade pumpkin spice 'latte' – and it's *EASY* ...

Similar to the method in Flavoured Coffee, add pumpkin pie seasoning to your coffee grounds before brewing. Once ready, pour a cup and leave space to include some heavy whipping cream. Add a little sugar – Simple!

Thanks, Eryn!

RUSSIAN TEA

This was a popular hot beverage in the 1960s.
Groovy ... let's bring it back!

As I changed the direction of Whidbey Island Baking Company from production baking to writing baking books, a number of friends volunteered some of their favourite recipes for me to include. My friend, Eryn, shared her recipe for instant Russian Tea. I had never heard of it before. When I looked into this tea, I learned how tea came to Europe, the culture of tea that developed in Russia, ultimately why this Russian Tea mimicked actual Russian tea and had particular popularity in the 1960s.

U.S. STANDARD – METRIC	INGREDIENT
1 jar (1Lb 4oz)	Orange flavoured powdered drink mix
2/3 cup – 160 ml	Instant Iced Tea
1/4 cup – 60 ml	Lemonade Mix
1 teaspoon – 5 ml	Cinnamon
1 teaspoon – 5 ml	Ground Cloves

PREPARATION & SERVING
Simple! Combine all the ingredients in a large bowl and mix thoroughly. Store your mixture in a sealed container – a glass jar looks especially nice. To serve, boil water and mix to taste similar to hot chocolate.

TIPS & THOUGHTS
You may wish to play around with the proportions of the ingredients to find what you prefer. Some instant Russian Tea recipes include sugar – I suggest instead leaving this for the individual to sweeten to taste using sugar, honey, sugar substitute, or any of the other options available.

Make an alternate batch using caffeine-free instant tea – and if you are serving this to kids, they won't know the difference. Fill jars with your mixture – it makes an instant (pun partly intended) gift from your kitchen. Fill a travel-ready container and enjoy some instant Russian Tea wherever you go.

One fall day as my editor, Linda, was working her way through my book she sent me an unexpected message. She has a recipe called Friendship Tea, and it is very similar to Russian Tea. To make Friendship Tea, simply make the Russian Tea recipe above with the addition of 1 teaspoon each of allspice and nutmeg, 2/3rds teaspoon cardamom, and 1 more teaspoon of cinnamon. *Thanks, Linda!*

PAIRINGS
A cold morning when you want a cozy beverage to cuddle up with...

Times that you want something tasty as an alternative to your usual favourite hot beverage...

When a friend is visiting and you want to introduce them to something they probably have not had before...

Rainy days reading a cherished book relaxing on a couch...

BLUEBERRY BUCKLE

As a kid, it was always a special Sunday morning when my mom would make Blueberry Buckle – now I share it with friends when they visit my home. Not until working on this cookbook did I find out that many years ago this recipe was given to my mom by our next door neighbor – Dorothy, wherever you are, *Thank You!*

TOPPING

U.S. STANDARD – METRIC	INGREDIENT
2 Tablespoons – 30 ml	Unsalted Butter
1/2 cup – 120 ml	Brown Sugar, packed
1/3 cup – 80 ml	All-Purpose Flour
	Cinnamon

BATTER

U.S. STANDARD – METRIC	INGREDIENT
4 Tablespoons – 60 ml	Unsalted Butter
3/4 cup – 180 ml	White Sugar
1	Large Egg
1 teaspoon – 5 ml	Pure Vanilla Extract
1/2 cup – 120 ml	Milk
2 teaspoons – 10 ml	Baking Powder
2 cup – 480 ml	All-Purpose Flour

2 cup – 480 ml ....Frozen Blueberries

MIXING – TOPPING
1. Using a fork and mixing bowl, combine butter, brown sugar, and flour; season with cinnamon to taste.
2. Press ingredients together until blended and set aside.

MIXING – BATTER
1. Heat oven to 375° F/190° C/Gas Mark 5.
2. Cream butter, white sugar, egg, and vanilla extract.
3. Alternately add milk, baking powder, and flour.
4. Fold in frozen blueberries. Work quickly from here forward to keep the blueberries from thawing.
5. Spread batter into a 9 x 9 inch square pan, then crumble topping evenly on top.
6. Bake at for 35 minutes.

Cut in 6 to 9 even pieces and serve fresh – warm or cool. Store in a tightly sealed container.

TIPS & THOUGHTS
If you want the topping to be chewier, increase the brown sugar.

If you prefer a topping with a bit more crumble to it try this...
4 Tablespoons – 60 ml ....Unsalted Butter
1/2 cup – 120 ml...Quick Oats
1/4 cup – 60 ml...Brown or White Sugar
1/3 cup – 80 ml...All-Purpose Flour
1 Tablespoons – 15 ml ....Cinnamon

If for some reason this coffee cake does not bake right – and I predict that the problem would be that this comes out of the oven over-moist in the center – try again. Attempt the recipe with a slight adjustment – instead bake at 350° F/180° C/Gas Mark 4 for 40 to 45 minutes.

I have had thoughts about experimenting with this recipe – *thoughts*, but I have not done much. Blackberry Buckle sounds good to me, and I am sure there are other possible combinations. A couple of years ago I attempted turning this recipe into an Apple Fritter Coffee Cake. Obviously, for it to be a 'fritter' it would have to be fried. However, I like the idea of having the characteristics of an apple fritter as a healthier baked good. Once I perfect my recipe, I will release it in one of my books.

PAIRINGS
Coffee, tea, hot cocoa for the kids, friends, and family!

EASY SLOW COOKER APPLESAUCE

Imagine how good it will feel to make and serve your own homemade applesauce ...

I enjoy applesauce as part of my breakfast. After having some applesauce my mom made, I might never purchase a commercial product again.

SUPPLIES
Slow Cooker, Peeler, Paring knife, Potato masher or Blender

INGREDIENTS
Apples, Apple Juice or Water, Brown Sugar, and Cinnamon or other spices

DIRECTIONS
1. Add about a 1/2 inch/12 millimeters water or juice to your crock pot.
2. Add cinnamon to taste along with any other spices you might like. For a 3.5 quart/3360 milliliters slow cooker add about 1/4 to 1/2 cup/60 to 120 milliliters brown sugar – personally, I just

eyeball it ... so for a larger pot I guess you just open your eyes wider?
3. Peel, core, and quarter enough apples to loosely fill your crock pot.
4. Cook on a low setting for several hours until the apple chunks are soft.
5. Mash the soften chunks by hand or put through a blender.

Serve warm or cool. Store in a sealed container and refrigerate.

TIPS & THOUGHTS
When I first made applesauce in my slow cooker I used gleaned apples that I had been given. They were small and odd shaped, but free is a great price. I have not compared the difference between making my own applesauce and buying it off the shelf. However, it did seem that there were some savings. I would have also saved a lot of time with regular sized apples. It felt good to make applesauce myself and to know exactly what went into it – I also enjoyed the creative process. Try experimenting with various types and combinations of apples to get a flavour you like.

For an extra tasty touch, add a few teaspoons of pure vanilla extract toward the end of the cooking. Pure almond and raspberry extracts are also good options. I have also used different juices – cranberry, pomegranate, and grape – while these add a dimension, it also makes the applesauce a little darker.

Don't have any juice on hand? A couple of packets of hot apple cider along with some water will do just as well.

If you are dealing with an abundant supply of apples, as with harvest season, there are a few ways you can prolong storage and be ahead on applesauce. The easiest is simply to freeze it. My mom fills sealable freezer bags and carefully places them in her freezer. I like to fill mason jars and put on a ring and lid or one of the newer plastic lids. Be sure your applesauce has fully cooled before doing this, and keep in mind expansion when freezing – but in my experience, applesauce does not seem to expand much and it also thaws quickly. Another option, which takes a little more work, would be to can your applesauce. This provides long-term storage and only takes space in your pantry instead of your freezer. If you are unfamiliar with how to can food, go online as there are many excellent tutorials and groups that will show you the supplies you will need and teach you how to can. Remember – the three things that make food go bad are air, heat, and light – so seal and store in a cool dark place.

When mashing the apples – if you use a potato masher or any other type of metal implement – *be careful*. Vigorous mashing or other action can damage the ceramic finish of a slow cooker pot. Be gentle, your crock pot will appreciate it.

MAIN COURSES

| Cheeseburger Soup | Chicken Bacon Burger Soup | Incredible Baked Ziti | Simple Pulled Pork | Taco Soup |

FAMILY

When I was young there was one meal at our house that was sacred – *dinner*. Between work for my dad and older sister and school for my younger sister and me, breakfast and lunch were always catch-as-catch-can. When it came to dinner the whole family would always gather around the table to eat and to talk about our day. Nothing could interfere with that meal. We didn't have a lot of money, but mom always did her best to serve us a filling and nutritious meal often with minimal ingredients.

When people think of "comfort foods" they usually remember something they enjoyed when they weren't feeling well or had had a bad day. For me they are many of the meals we had when I was a kid around our dinner table. Often, our dinner was a filling and delicious soup. One of my favorites was Cheeseburger Soup. Mom had an amazing ability to stretch a pound or so of ground beef, cheese, some veggies and potatoes into a wonderful meal to feed and satisfy five people and the occasional neighborhood friend who happened by.

Mom was very spare with sharing her recipes. Sometimes they were just in her head, but the ones that were recorded on paper were often "missing" some key ingredients. My wife, Chris, and I spent some time recreating those comforting meals for our own enjoyment and rediscovering those lost ingredients to get the flavors I remembered. One of those recreations will be found in this section. Give these recipes a try and maybe they will become comfort foods for you and your family as well.

Arne ~ New York, USA

CHRIS & ARNE'S FABULOUS CHEESEBURGER SOUP

When I posted online that I was merely *considering* taking recipe submissions to include in my book an interesting thing happened ... within the next five minutes I received six recipes from four different people. What great support!
This is one of those recipes – *Thanks, Chris & Arne!*

U.S. STANDARD – METRIC	INGREDIENT
1/2 Lb – 230 g	Ground Beef
3/4 cup – 180 ml	Chopped Onion
3/4 cup – 180 ml	Carrots, Shredded or Sliced
3/4 cup – 180 ml	Diced Celery
1 teaspoon – 5 ml	Dried Basil
1 teaspoon – 5 ml	Dried Parsley
4 Tablespoons – 60 ml	Butter
3 cups – 720 ml	Chicken Broth
4 cups – 960 ml	Diced, Peeled Potatoes
1/4 cup – 60 ml	Flour
8 to 16 Oz – 230 to 460 g	American Cheese, Cubed
1 1/2 cups – 360 ml	Milk
3/4 teaspoon – 3.7 ml	Salt
1/4 to 1/2 teaspoon – 1.25 to 2.5 ml	Ground Black Pepper
1/4 cup – 60 ml	Sour Cream

TOPPINGS (Optional)
- Bacon-bits or bacon cut into dime-sized pieces
- Small chunks of ham
- Shredded cheese
- More Sour cream

DIRECTIONS
1. In a large skillet, brown the ground beef and drain. Set the beef aside.

2. In the same skillet, add a little butter and sauté onions, carrot, and celery until tender. Add basil and parsley towards the end of the cooking.
3. In a large soup pan, add the chicken broth, potatoes, and ground beef and bring to a boil. Reduce the heat to a simmer, cover and let cook until the potatoes are fork tender.
4. In a separate pan, melt the 4 Tablespoons butter over medium heat, add the flour and cook for 3 or 4 minutes or until the roux starts to turn a pale blonde color. Add some of the hot liquid from the soup pot to the roux and then return the roux to the soup pot.
5. Bring soup to a boil to thicken, stirring to prevent lumps. Boil for two minutes and then reduce heat to a simmer. Add vegetables. Add cheese and SLOWLY pour in the milk. Add salt and pepper to taste. When cheese is incorporated into the soup, remove from the heat.
6. Whisk in the sour cream.
7. Serve with toppings.

Serves 4-5 people. Refrigerate leftovers in a sealed container.

TIPS & THOUGHTS
Monterey Jack, Colby, Swiss or other cheeses may be added or substituted to taste. You can also add more cheese or ground beef to the recipe to taste.

PAIRINGS
So here's the thing about Chris & Arne's Fabulous Cheeseburger Soup ...

The first time I made it was only weeks before publishing this book. I had already made the next recipe in this chapter, which I developed and gave namesake to Arne and his wife Chris (she's an *AMAZING* baker by-the-way), and there was no doubt in my mind that this recipe would be good, too. It's not just good – it's *GREAT!* When it came to the Pairings for this soup, I figured to ask Arne – while working on this book on my laptop I sent him a message – here's his response...

"We usually whip up a large batch of soup in fall/winter, enough to last a few meals. It is very warming on those cold winter evenings. But, frankly, the Fabulous Cheeseburger Soup is *WAY* too good to share, although we have been known to serve it to family and good friends. Hot soup on a cold evening is such a nice combination. It's warming for the body and soul."

CHRIS & ARNE'S FABULOUS CHICKEN-BACON BURGER SOUP

Directions for stovetop or slow cooker...

Shortly after receiving the recipe for Chris & Arne's Fabulous Cheeseburger Soup, a friend whom I had not seen in some time happened to drop by. We got to visiting and as the day progressed, I realized I was going to need to come up with dinner. Using ingredients I had on hand, I realized I could make Chris & Arne's soup flavoured as a different sandwich on a grill menu. My friend and I rolled up our sleeves and got to work in the kitchen as we continued to visit. It was pleasant cooking together while we reconnected, and we ended up enjoying a great dinner. The next day I emailed my recipe to Chris & Arne, and it only seemed fitting that I gave them the credit. In music terms I would say that it's their tune, I just arranged it.

U.S. STANDARD – METRIC	INGREDIENT
1/2 Lb – 230 g	Cooked Chicken
3/4 cup – 180 ml	Chopped Onion
3/4 cup – 180 ml	Carrots, Shredded or Sliced
3/4 cup – 180 ml	Diced Celery
1 teaspoon – 5 ml	Dried Basil (optional)
1 teaspoon – 5 ml	Dried Parsley (optional)
3 cups – 720 ml	Chicken Broth
4 cups – 960 ml	Diced, Peeled Potatoes
4 Tablespoons – 60 ml	Butter
1/4 cup – 60 ml	Flour
8 to 16 Oz – 230 to 460 g	American Cheese, Cubed
1 1/2 cups – 360 ml	Milk
3/4 teaspoon – 3.7 ml	Salt
1/4 to 1/2 teaspoon – 1.25 to 2.5 ml	Ground Black Pepper
1/4 cup – 60 ml	Sour Cream

TOPPINGS (Optional)

- Bacon-bits or bacon cut into dime-sized pieces
- Small chunks of ham
- Shredded cheese

- More Sour cream

DIRECTIONS – STOVETOP
1. Cube cooked chicken and set aside.
2. Melt a little butter in a skillet and sauté onions, carrot, and celery until tender. Add basil and parsley towards the end of the cooking.
3. In a large soup pan, add the chicken broth, potatoes, and cubed chicken and bring to a boil. Reduce the heat to a simmer, cover and let cook until the potatoes are fork tender.
4. In a separate pan, melt the 4 Tablespoons/60 mL butter over medium heat, add the flour and cook for 3 or 4 minutes or until the roux starts to turn a pale blonde color. Add some of the hot liquid from the soup pot to the roux and then return the roux to the soup pot.
5. Bring soup to a boil to thicken, stirring to prevent lumps. Boil for two minutes and then reduce heat to a simmer. Add sautéed vegetables. Add cheese and milk. Add salt and pepper to taste. When cheese is incorporated into the soup, remove from the heat.
6. Whisk in the sour cream.
7. Serve with toppings.

DIRECTIONS – SLOW COOKER
1. Cube the cooked chicken and set it aside.
2. Heat 1 cup of chicken broth and keep nearby. Melt 4 Tablespoons/60 mL butter in a pan over medium heat. Add the flour and cook for 3 or 4 minutes or until the roux starts to turn a pale blonde color. Add some of the hot broth to the roux and then pour all of the roux into the slow cooker pot.
3. Sauté the onions, carrot, and celery and add them to the slow cooker along with the basil and parsley. Optionally, you can skip the sautéing and just add these to the slow cooker.
4. Pour the rest of the chicken broth into the slow cooker along with potatoes and chicken and put on low for 6 to 8 hours, cooking until the potatoes are fork tender.
5. Over time the soup will boil which will help to thicken it. Occasional stirring every few hours will help to prevent lumps. About an hour before serving switch the temp to low. Add

cheese and slowly stir in the milk. Add salt and pepper to taste. When cheese is incorporated into the soup, remove from the heat and whisk in the sour cream.
6. Serve with toppings.

Serves 4-5 people. Refrigerate leftovers in a sealed container.

TIPS & THOUGHTS
Blue Cheese crumble, Monterey Jack, Colby, Swiss or other cheeses may be added or substituted to taste. You can also add more cheese and more chicken or ham to the recipe to taste.

When cutting up and cooking things like potatoes and carrots, I was taught to try and make the pieces the same size – this is supposed to help them to cook evenly.

This is an obvious idea – try switching the chicken for turkey. Would that make this Chris & Arne's Fabulous Turkey-Bacon Wrap Soup?

PAIRINGS
After my first experience with this recipe ... friends & loved ones, *Of Course!*

INCREDIBLE BAKED ZITI

Think of this like lasagna – SIMPLIFIED!

Please be aware that you, your friends, and family will probably CONSUME THIS IN MASS QUANTITIES!!!
Why – because *IT'S TASTY*.

U.S. STANDARD – METRIC	INGREDIENT
16 ounces – 460 g	Italian Sausage
16 ounces – 460 g	Ziti or other small pasta
3-4 Tablespoons – 45-60 ml	Pesto
	Basil and Pine Nuts (optional)
16 ounces – 460 g	Low-Fat Ricotta Cheese Cottage Cheese
36 ounces – 1.06 l	Spaghetti Sauce
16 ounces – 460 g	Shredded Mozzarella Cheese

TOPPINGS (Optional)
Grated Parmesan cheese, sour cream

INSTRUCTIONS
1. Cook the sausage as directed or in a frying pan over medium-low heat; drain when ready.
2. Cook and drain the pasta as instructed.
3. Mix the pesto into the ricotta cheese.
4. Heat your oven to 350° F/175° C/Gas Mark 4.
5. Pour only enough spaghetti sauce into a 9 x 13 inch casserole dish to cover the bottom – for easier clean-up you may wish to coat your dish with cooking spray or aluminum foil first. Follow with layers of sausage, ricotta-pesto mixture, pasta, mozzarella, and sauce. Repeat as many times as needed until the dish is full or you have used up the ingredients. Reserve enough mozzarella to cover the top of the last layer completely. If any pasta is exposed, cover the dish with foil before baking as this will help to keep the pasta from drying out.
6. Bake for 50-60 minutes.

7. Remove your dish from the oven and if necessary remove the foil. Top with mozzarella and return dish to the oven. Broil for 2-4 minutes or bake 6-10 minutes or until the mozzarella is bubbly and golden-brown.

Cover or store in a sealed container and refrigerate ... Although, I doubt that you will have leftovers.

TIPS & THOUGHTS

When I was introduced to Baked Ziti, it was made with penne instead of ziti. I know... you, like me, sit around all day gripped with stress contemplating the meaning of life, the universe, and everything – and that 'everything' includes the important things like the difference between ziti and penne. Frankly, most people *Do Not Know Or Care* – and had I not been introduced to Baked Ziti I would not be aware of the distinction – and here it is ...

> *These two noodles are basically the same*
> *except that*
> *penne has ridges on the outside and ziti does not.*

There you go, now you can rest peacefully at night knowing that your life is complete. When it comes to this recipe, toe-may-toe/toe-mah-toh, ziti or penne, either will do. Use rotini or any small shaped pasta – spaghetti broken up into small pieces would work although it has less visual appeal . Really, use whatever floats your ferry.

The measurements with this recipe are loose – do what tastes good to you. If your spaghetti sauce is not already seasoned, you will probably want to add flavour – use garlic, herbs, Italian seasoning, or other additions that you enjoy. Including a chopped onion would be good. Whole-milk ricotta may be used, however considering the amount of cheese this recipe calls for, low-fat ricotta may be a preferred choice. The basil and pine nut with the pesto is optional ... but yummy. Yes, I said 'yummy.'

PAIRINGS

Hungry people who enjoy good food – give 'em a big salad, too!

SIMPLE SLOW COOKER PULLED PORK

U.S. STANDARD – METRIC	INGREDIENT
3 to 4 pounds – 1.361 to 1.814 kg	Boneless Pork Shoulder
2 cups – 475 ml	Chicken or Beef Broth
18 oz – 510 g	Barbecue Sauce Bottle
	Seasoning Salt, to taste
	Liquid smoke, to taste

DIRECTIONS for a 3.5-quart slow cooker
1. Rinse pork and place in your slow cooker. Shake on some seasoning salt and douse with 3-6 capfuls liquid smoke (about 2 to 4 teaspoons). Add broth and cook on low for 8 hours.
2. Remove pork from the slow cooker and place on a large cutting board followed by draining the liquid from the slow cooker. Gently detach meat sections so that you may remove the fat and non-meat elements. Place the meat back in the slow cooker.
3. Add the same amount of seasoning salt and liquid smoke and the whole bottle of barbecue sauce. Pull apart (shred) the meat using 2 forks.
4. Cook for 30-60 minutes on high.

Serves 4-5 people. Refrigerate leftovers in a sealed container.

TIPS & THOUGHTS
While this recipe calls for 3 to 4 pounds of meat, I have used as much as 5 pounds/2.25 kilograms in my 3.5-quart slow cooker, and it seems to cook in the same amount of time. Alternatively, I have used the same amount of chicken – this only takes 4 to 6 hours for the primary cooking and the meat is easier to clean.

Of course, if you do not have chicken or beef broth, water with bouillon cubes will work equally well. You may opt to drain the liquid after the initial cooking into a storage container as this may be cooled, frozen, and reused later as the base for some tasty stew – why waste a good thing?

When you shred the meat using the two forks, do your best to avoid the ceramic finish of your slow cooker – the metal and shredding action can cause damage to the bowl. Optionally you may prefer to shred the meat on your cutting board. Once the meat is back in the slow cooker pot, try to get the BBQ sauce spread around onto all of the meat.

Spring 2013 I experienced pulled pork 'done right' at a renowned BBQ restaurant in Savannah, Georgia. There the sandwich was served more like the meat before the second cooking in my recipe; a variety of BBQ sauces were available as table condiments. Frankly, I prefer my approach – it seems like less work, and the flavour can be tasted more thoroughly throughout the meat.

Usually pulled pork is served hot – and when it is, it's definitely comfort food. When it comes to leftovers, reheat some meat or make cold sandwiches. The beauty of cold sandwiches is that you can enjoy some pulled pork on-the-go!

PAIRINGS
I would encourage you to think of this as a relaxed lunch or dinner. Put the pulled pork on bread or buns and serve as sandwiches. Some people like to have garnishings like pickles or cheese with their sandwich – personally, I enjoy the contrast of a little ranch dressing. This would be well accompanied by coleslaw and a favourite beverage.

SLOW COOKER TACO SOUP

This filling Tex-Mex meal is tasty and fun. Let go of being *'proper'* when enjoying this soup – dress up your bowl with your favourite toppings, and crush the chips over the top or use them as scoops like when eating salsa.

U.S. STANDARD – METRIC	INGREDIENT
1 to 1 1/2 lbs – 452.8 to 679.2 g	Cooked Chicken
1/2 Large	White Onion, chopped
1 4 oz can – 113 g	Chopped Green Chilies
1 15 oz can – 425 g	Whole Kernel Corn
1 15 oz can – 425 g	Black Beans
1 1.25 oz envelope – 35 g	Taco Seasoning
1 15 oz can – 425 g	Tomato Sauce
1 15 oz can – 425 g	Diced Tomatoes
28 oz can – 850 g	Mexican Hominy

TOPPINGS
Corn chips, ranch dressing, shredded cheddar cheese, shredded lettuce, chopped tomato, and sour cream – some people like to use a little guacamole, too.

DIRECTIONS for a 3.5-quart slow cooker
1. Chop the chicken and onion put it in the slow cooker pot.
2. Drain the chopped green chilies and corn. Rinse and drain the black beans. Add these to pot.
3. Add the taco seasoning, tomato sauce, and diced tomatoes. Pour the entire can of hominy into slow cooker pot – yes, liquid included.
4. Stir the ingredients until well mixed. Set slow cooker on low and heat for 4 to 6 hours. Optionally, stir the pot about every two hours.
5. Once cooked turn off your slow cooker, uncover the pot, stir, and spoon into bowls. Serve and enjoy with desired toppings.

Serves 4-5 people. Refrigerate leftovers in a sealed container.

TIPS & THOUGHTS
As far as I'm concerned, this recipe ROCKS – it's tasty, considerably healthy, it is dead-easy to make, it's affordable, and it lasts for several meals.

I received this recipe from my mom, and I have since made a few modifications. Originally it called for 1.5 cups water after draining the hominy – why waste a good thing – the liquid in the can of hominy adds flavour. The recipe also called for a whole onion, which I cut down by half to be able to add the black beans. Using fire-roasted diced tomatoes adds a visual and flavour dimension. Ground beef may be used in place of chicken, which seems to make the soup spicier. I prefer this soup on the thick side, so a few days in advance of making the recipe I chop a whole onion and put it in my food drier – once combined and cooking, the dried onion absorbs moisture and makes the soup stew-like. Lime chips, over salted corn chips, are also tasty.

The order the ingredients go in does not matter as long as they all get in – just make sure to cook, drain or not drain everything as directed. This soup, of course, can also be prepared on a stove top in a soup pot if you need to shorten the time to serving. When preparing in a slow cooker, avoid frequent stirring or lifting the lid to smell the soup. *Leave It Alone* – each time the lid is removed the slow cooker takes about 15 minutes to get back up to temperature, thereby affecting the cook-time.

You may be able to cut down the cost of this recipe by using fresh or frozen ingredients. When I make this recipe, I usually use fresh chicken (which I bake) and frozen corn. A person could potentially reduce the expense by using fresh diced tomatoes and rehydrated black beans along with other cost-cutting ingredients.

Since most of the ingredients are available in canned form, I keep a few sets in my pantry for emergencies. I even store the dried onions portioned in sealed plastic bags. Whether I use my slow cooker, stove top when short on time, or a camp stove during a power outage, this soup is ready to go!

PAIRINGS
Friends!

HIGHLAND BAGPIPE SHEET MUSIC

| Beag air Bheag (Little by Little) | Lullaby for Zoe | Brother Emmett's Waltz |

FINALLY ... SOME MUSIC

"One ought, every day at least, to hear a little song, read a good poem, see a fine picture, and, if it were possible, to speak a few reasonable words."
Johann Wolfgang von Goethe ~ Germany

You have reached the end of my book. At this point you have baked some tasty cookies, rolled some biscotti, drank some delightful coffee, and enjoyed some comfort food with loved ones. So now all that's left ... is a little music!

You've probably never seen this in a recipe book before ...

BagpiperDon ~ Washington, USA

BEAG AIR BHEAG (LITTLE BY LITTLE)
Slow Air
© Don P. Scoby 11July2005

There is a very old Scottish tune titled "Togail Curs Air Leodhas" – or "Setting A Course For Lewis" – and it is one of my favourite pieces! As I have been taught about the lyric and lore of the song, in it a young man is encouraging the woman he loves to return with him to the Isle of Lewis, where they are both from, to announce their engagement. While romantic in content, this piece is among the Scottish work tunes and is a rowing song.

I wrote the following tune to be played as a compliment to Setting A Course For Lewis and titled it "Little by Little". I wanted its name to sound more traditional so I asked my friend, Rich, a Seattle area Gaelic instructor, for the translation – and "Beag air Bheag" was complete!

I originally composed Little by Little in July of 2005; my arrangement here was made 15November2016.

LULLABY FOR ZOË
Slow Waltz / Lullaby / Slow March
© *Don P. Scoby November 2008 & January 2009*

About a month after writing this tune I received a call from friends of mine. They just had their first child – a daughter – and they asked that I might be her surrogate uncle. I was honored to be asked, and of course I said *Yes*. I wanted to mark the occasion with a gift – however, being a broke musician I was unable to contribute something tangible to the beginning of her life. Then I remembered this melodic – *and previously untitled* – piece I had composed and dedicated it to my new niece.

I originally wrote "Lullaby For Zoë" on 01November2008 finishing at 2130hrs, then continued to arrange it finishing around 2250hrs. The second and final arrangements were 03January2009 and 10Jananuary2009 1406hrs.

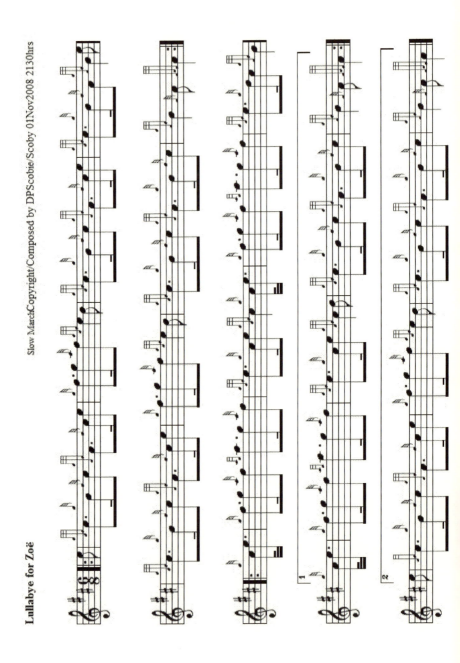

BROTHER EMMETT'S WALTZ
Waltz
© Don P. Scoby 06August2011 & 04October2011

A few years after I wrote "Lullaby For Zoë" I became interested in waltzes. As I found few within Highland bagpipe music, I experimented with composing my own. Terry Tully's waltz "The Ass In The Graveyard" had particularly grabbed me due to its 6/8 meter, texture, and lyrical attributes. One summer day something clicked in my creative mind – Lullaby For Zoë could speak with some of this same character.

About a week after I rearranged the lullaby into the following tune, I received a call from Zoë's dad telling me that she now had a brother named Emmett and asked that I would be his surrogate uncle, too. *Certainly, of course I would* – and as it would happen, the newly reworked piece would become the tune for my new nephew. As in life, Lullaby For Zoë and her Brother Emmett's Waltz are brother-sister tunes and they play nicely together.

Brother Emmett's

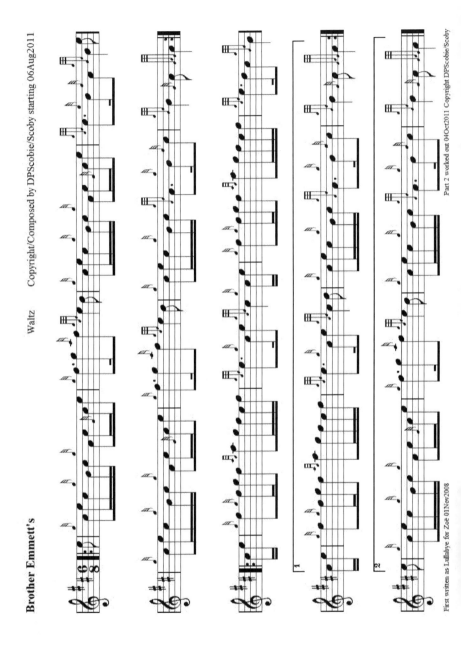

ABOUT THE AUTHOR

Donald P. Scoby has lived in the Pacific Northwest since birth and was raised cooking and baking with his parents and grandmother between Seattle and Whidbey Island. Now a full-time resident of 'The Rock', this debut book marks the new direction of Whidbey Island Baking Company and shares his passion for the baked goods he has imagined and created.

OTHER WORKS AND FUTURE WORK BY DON P. SCOBY

This marks my first foray into book publishing, adding to a small collection of music albums I have previously self-produced. I am already hard at work making additional books and other goods available. Please look for these products and more to come…

WHIDBEY ISLAND BAKING COMPANY
My previously in-production baking business turned into writing recipe books and more
Online
WhidbeyIslandBaking.com and on social media
Books Available Now
Make Your Own Darn Good Cookies
Cookies, Biscotti, Coffee, and Other Comfort Food
Coming Soon
Baking & Cooking Recipe Books, E-Books
Shirts, Aprons, Stickers and More

DONALD P. SCOBY
Coming Soon
Poetry, Children's Books, Fiction and Science Fiction
E-books, Audio Books, and Audio Book Narration
Backpack Patterns … yes, backpack patterns
Shirts

BAGPIPERDON

Professional Celtic Musician playing Highland Bagpipes, Scottish Smallpipes, and Bodhrán
Recording Artist, Scottish Bagpipe Instructor, and sometimes Singer

Online
BagpiperDon.com and on social media

Coming Soon
Highland Bagpipe and Scottish Smallpipe Albums
Sheet Music Books for Scottish Bagpipes including my Compositions & Arrangements along with works by Guest Composers

NAE REGRETS

Celtic Rock … sometimes with Bellydancers!

Online
NaeRegrets.com and on social media

Albums Available Now
Alive at Northwest Folklife 2009

Coming Soon
More albums, more performances … and more bellydancers?
Band Shirts, Stickers and other products
Widdendream with Ceòl gu Brath re-release double EP
In Memory of Decibel Celt

ARCHIVE OF RESONANCE

Experiential Recordings & Creative Projects

Online
ArchiveOfResonance.com and on social media

Albums Available Now
Wind & Harps

Albums Coming Soon
Water Drums
Thunder & Hard Rain
Freedom Ride (Motorcycle Rally)
Hummingbirds

NOTES

NOTES

AND MORE NOTES

DRAW A PICTURE

LEAVE THIS PAGE BLANK

DON'T FOLLOW DIRECTIONS
–
DO SOMETHING CREATIVE ON THE PRECEDING PAGE

THIS BOOK IS A PREVIEW
OF THINGS TO COME

I HOPE YOU WILL ENJOY IT
FOR MANY YEARS

AND FIND ALL THE HIDDEN BITS

42

All your base are belong to us.

Made in the USA
Columbia, SC
13 December 2019